AMAZING DISCOVERIES
THAT UNLOCK THE
BIBLE

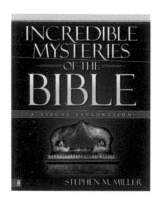

Incredible Mysteries of the Bible
Stephen M. Miller
ISBN-13: 978-0-310-25594-9
ISBN-10: 0-310-25594-5

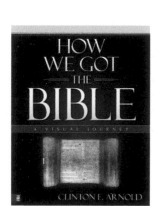

How We Got the Bible
Clinton E. Arnold
ISBN-13: 978-0-310-25306-8
ISBN-10: 0-310-25306-3

AMAZING DISCOVERIES
THAT UNLOCK THE
BIBLE

A VISUAL EXPERIENCE

DOUGLAS CONNELLY

ZONDERVAN®

ZONDERVAN

Amazing Discoveries That Unlock the Bible
Copyright © 2008 by Douglas Connelly

Requests for information should be addressed to:
Zondervan, *Grand Rapids, Michigan 49530*

Library of Congress Cataloging-in-Publication Data

Connelly, Douglas, 1949 –
    Amazing discoveries that unlock the Bible : a visual experience / Douglas Connelly.
      p. cm. – (Zondervan visual reference series)
      ISBN-13: 978-0-310-25799-8
      ISBN-10: 0-310-25799-9
    1. Bible—Antiquities 2. Middle East—Antiquities 3. Middle East—Civilization. 4. Europe—Antiquites. 5. Europe—Civilization. I. Title.
BS621.C625 2007
220.9′3—dc22

2007000424

Interior design by Ron Huizenga

Printed in The United States of America

22 23 24 25 26 27 28 29 30 31 32 33 34 35 36 37 38 39 40 /TRM/ 22 21 20 19 18 17 16 15 14 13 12 11 10 9 8 7 6 5 4 3 2

TABLE OF CONTENTS

► **THE PLACE** overlooking the Sea of Galilee where Jesus delivered the Sermon on the Mount (Matthew 5–7).

DIGGING UP THE BIBLE

The events of the Bible took place in history—in real places with real people. But the nations, armies, and rulers of the Bible along with the musicians, carpenters, and school teachers passed off the scene long ago. What was their world like?

Archaeology helps us reconstruct the biblical world. The study of ancient things (which is what the word archaeology means) involves knowledge of history, geography, language, money, warfare, biology, ceramics, and even medicine. Scholars may sift carefully through the ruins of a city or a burial site or even a garbage dump. They use highly sophisticated methods of excavation, soil analysis, carbon dating, and photography. It's a very detailed, difficult job! But once in a while, the diggers and discoverers come upon an object or building or piece of writing so startling, so amazing that it makes all the hard work seem like nothing.

In this book, we will look at some of the most amazing discoveries about the Bible ever made—and we will see how those discoveries unlock God's Word. It's a journey you won't forget!

► **BUST OF AUGUSTUS CAESAR**, ruler of the Roman Empire when Jesus was born.

▲ GOLDEN BOWL from the
Canaanite city of Ugarit.

◀ A snapshot in
stone of the Persian
king, Xerxes, the royal
husband of Esther.
Xerxes ruled a a vast
empire that stretched from
India to Ethiopia.

▲ A SCROLL of the Psalms found
among the Dead Sea Scrolls.

DO THESE DISCOVERIES PROVE THE BIBLE IS TRUE?

▲ An image of the Caananite god, Baal.

Inscriptions on ancient memorial stones and long forgotten coins will never "prove" or "disprove" the Bible. Even if every historical fact was proven beyond question, the heart of the Bible's message must be accepted by faith. The discoveries of archaeology help us in other ways.

Archaeological discoveries demonstrate the accuracy of the biblical writers. As new documents are found or as new artifacts are uncovered, the reliability of the biblical record is confirmed over and over.

Evidence from the ancient world helps us better understand the cultural and historical context of the Bible. We learn how people lived and worked and thought. We can enter into their world and understand God's message more clearly.

Archaeology helps us unravel some of the riddles of the Bible. Political or historical questions are often resolved by examining related documents or surprising discoveries from the biblical world.

The people of the Bible come alive in our thinking. When we see the ankle of a crucified man or the prison where Paul was in chains or an object from Herod's magnificent temple, the biblical accounts take on new life.

Archaeology affirms our confidence in the Bible's truthfulness but, in the end, we trust in the living God as the source of truth, not in some relic from the past.

► THE SEAL READS, "Belonging to Jehoahaz, son of the king," and pictures a fighting rooster. Scholars aren't sure who Jehoahaz was—probably a lesser son of one of Israel's kings.

▲ A carved ivory box found at Megiddo.

◀ Carefully sifting through the dirt, destruction, and debris of an ancient site requires patience and tedious labor. Every significant artifact is photographed, catalogued, and meticulously preserved for further study.

SLAVE TAG

This Roman slave tag was attached to an iron collar and asks that the slave be returned to his owner. Runaway slaves (like Onesimus in Paul's letter to Philemon) were routinely collared to prevent further escape attempts. Persistent runaways were branded on the foreheads—an *F* for *fugitivus* (fugitive).

◀ **A JAR** like the ones the Dead Sea Scrolls were stored in. The dry climate around the Dead Sea preserved the leather scrolls for more than 2,000 years.

▲ Michelangelo's depiction of the flood on the ceiling of the Sistine Chapel in Rome.

THE BABYLONIAN FLOOD STORY

You've heard the story of Noah and the ark since you were a child, but what if you found another flood story from another culture and in an ancient language? George Smith, a British explorer and language specialist, found just such a story—and it caused a worldwide sensation. Smith was in the British Museum sifting through clay tablets recovered from the library of the Assyrian king, Ashurbanipal, when he came across an incredible passage. He found himself translating a flood story very much like the biblical account of Noah and the flood. He was so excited that he raised money to return to Nineveh in order to find the rest of the tablets—and amazingly he did!

The Babylonian flood story is told on the eleventh tablet of a much longer poem called the Epic of Gilgamesh. You can read the whole poem online or checked out from your local library. Gilgamesh apparently was a real king in the ancient land of Sumer (2700–2500 BC). Legends grew up around this heroic king and eventually the story became one of the culture's great epics. Does this Babylonian epic give us a better account of the flood than the Bible? No way! The Babylonian version is simply a corrupted memory of the actual flood, and that account is preserved accurately in Genesis 6–9.

◄ **SEVENTH-CENTURY BC TABLET** in which Utnaphishtim, the Babylonian "Noah," and his wife tell Gilgamesh about their experience in the great deluge.

CAPTION Text

AMAZING FLOOD STORIES

The Babylonian flood story is not the only account of that event outside the Bible. More than 200 flood legends have been found in cultures all over the world. In the ancient Greek legend, the heroes Deucalion and his wife Pyrrha entered the ark and the god Zeus sent nine days of such torrential rain that it carved out the present-day Greek peninsula. The Toltec Indians of ancient Mexico believed that a flood destroyed the world 1,716 years after its creation. Only a few people escaped in a closed wooden chest.

The legends are so numerous and from such diverse cultures that they could not have been simply copied from each other. Furthermore, the legends were recorded long before missionaries brought any knowledge of the biblical account of the flood to these cultures. James Perloff makes some startling comparisons: In 95 percent of the more than two hundred flood legends, the flood was worldwide; in 88 percent a certain family was chosen to survive; in 70 percent survival was by means of a boat or raft; in 67 percent animals were also saved; in 66 percent the flood was due to human sin and wickedness; and in 57 percent the boat came to rest on a mountain.*

▲ *Deucalion and Pyyrah are warned by Zeus to escape the coming flood.*

◄ **A STONE DEPICTION OF GILGAMESH,** the heroic king of Uruk in the land of the Sumerians. Gilgamesh learned the flood story as he traveled through the underworld and talked with the survivors of that long ago catastrophe.

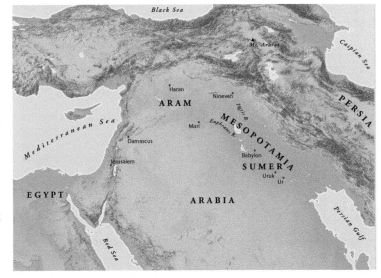

▲ The mountains of Ararat where the Bible says Noah's ark eventually came to rest—and where explorers have searched ever since for remains of a wooden ark.

PUABI'S HEADDRESS

In one burial chamber in Ur, a woman's skeleton was found with this elaborate headdress around her skull. The piece is made of lapis lazuli, carnelian, and gold leaves hammered to paper thinness, and resembles a blossoming tree. It is as strikingly beautiful now as when it was made forty-five centuries ago. Near the woman's body was a small clay cylinder identifying her as Puabi, one of the queens of Ur. The discoverers also found the remains of twelve young women in the chamber—servants and companions traveling with the queen to another world. Perhaps biblical Sarah, still considered beautiful at sixty-five years of age, adorned herself with similar jewelry.

▶ ONE OF THE FINEST pieces of art found in Ur is this figure of a goat decorated with gold, silver, lapis lazuli, and shells. This "ram caught in a thicket" is a reminder of God's provision of a ram that Abraham offered in the place of his son, Isaac (Genesis 22:13).

ROYAL TREASURES OF UR

▲ Ur was the center of the worship of the moon god, Nanna (called Sin by later Babylonians). This brick temple tower, called a ziggurat, dedicated to that god may resemble the original Tower of Babel with the top representing heaven as the place of direct contact with the god.

When God called Abraham to leave the ancient city of Ur and go to a new land, Abraham left behind a magnificent, highly cultured city to follow God into the unknown. Sir Leonard Woolley, a British explorer, uncovered hundreds of tombs at the site of the city of Ur. Sixteen of the tombs were spectacular—tombs of the kings. The treasures that filled the tombs had been buried for 4500 years but they opened our eyes to the splendor of a long-vanished culture, the same culture that nurtured young Abraham.

In one royal tomb, the burial place of the Sumerian king A-bar-gi, dozens of bodies crowded the ramp leading to the main burial chamber. Skeletons of oxen were found along with the remains of guards with spears and helmets. The bodies were so neatly placed that the excavators concluded the people had walked to their places, lay down, and drunk poison from a cup. Undertakers had made the final arrangement of the bodies and sealed the tomb. The king had gone to the afterworld surrounded by sixty servants, the same assistants who had cared for his needs in this world. The king's wife, Queen Shubad, died later and was buried above the king with a smaller group of only twenty-five servants.

◀ This banner is a mosaic of red limestone, shell, and blue lapis lazuli. One side shows a war scene; this side shows the victory feast and the parade of booty.

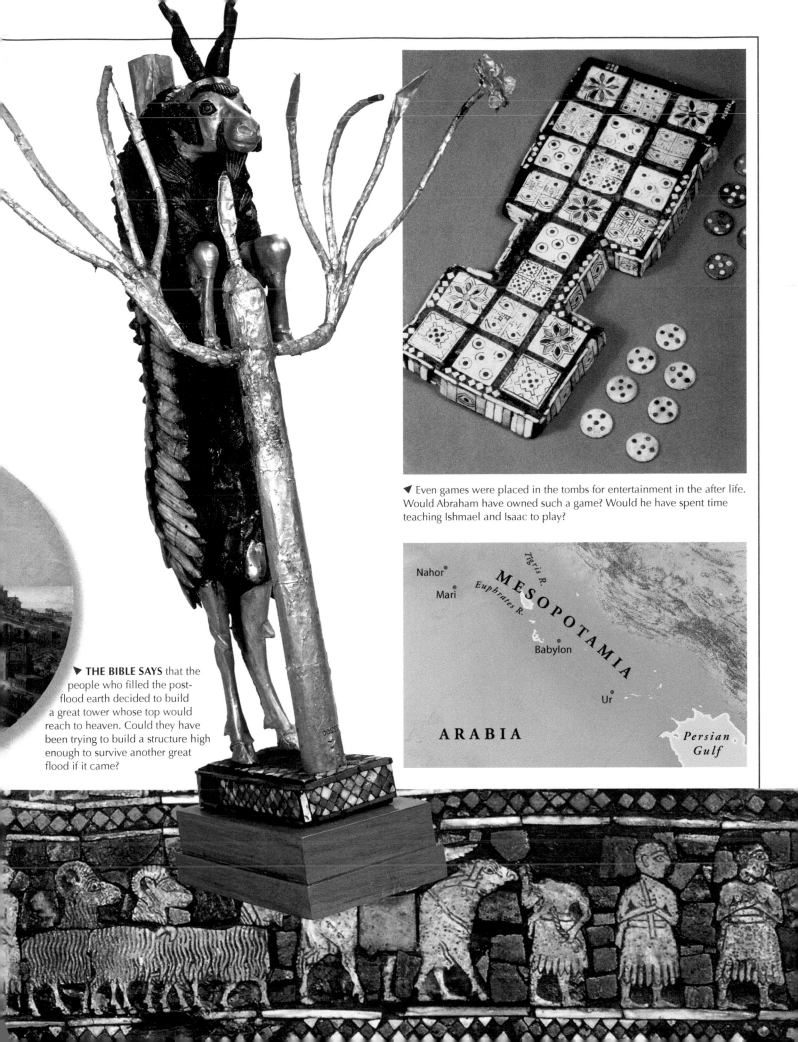

◀ Even games were placed in the tombs for entertainment in the after life. Would Abraham have owned such a game? Would he have spent time teaching Ishmael and Isaac to play?

Nahor
Mari
Tigris R.
MESOPOTAMIA
Euphrates R.
Babylon
Ur
ARABIA
Persian Gulf

▼ THE BIBLE SAYS that the people who filled the post-flood earth decided to build a great tower whose top would reach to heaven. Could they have been trying to build a structure high enough to survive another great flood if it came?

EBLA: LIVING LIKE A CANAANITE

Tel Mardikh is the mound covering the buried city of Ebla.

At first the claims were astonishing. A team of Italian scholars had made a major discovery in Syria. They had uncovered Ebla, the site of an ancient Canaanite kingdom that had existed at the time of Abraham and had lasted more than 800 years! What added to the excitement was the discovery of thousands of clay tablets in a new language.

The first reports in the 1970s sent shock waves through the Christian community. Biblical names like Adam, Ishmael, Esau, Saul, and even David were said to appear in the texts, confirming the use of such names in the region of Canaan. The discovery team claimed to find the name of the city of Jerusalem—a reference one thousand years earlier than any other we had. The cities of Sodom and Gomorrah were mentioned, sending scholars scrabbling, especially those who had denied such cities had ever existed.

Most of the sensational news has since been toned down. Archaeologists unfamiliar with this newly discovered language made claims that couldn't be supported under more careful examination. Ebla remains, however, a key discovery for the era of the earliest ancestors of the people of Israel. We can learn a lot about Abraham's world and even about how the Hebrew language developed. Long lists of zoological, geographic, and even mathematical terms have yet to be fully translated and understood. Undoubtedly the proverbs and business contracts and grocery lists at Ebla will help us understand the biblical languages better in the years ahead. The highly publicized "proof" of the Bible, however, was not a realistic expectation.

Human-headed (and fully bearded) bull discovered in the ruins of Ebla.

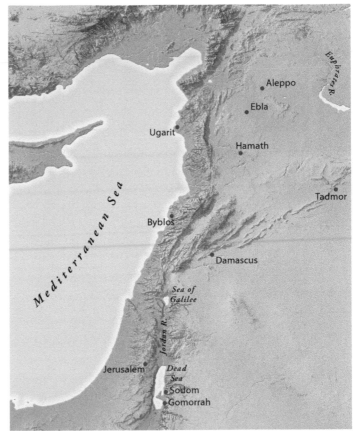

▲ **17,000 CLAY TABLETS** were discovered at Ebla—four times more than all the previous texts from this time period. When fire destroyed the palace, the heat baked the clay tablets and preserved them for thousands of years. The documents reveal a powerful city-state of about 200,000 inhabitants, noted for its exports of textiles, wood, and fine metals.

▲ Salt deposits around the Dead Sea remind us of Lot's wife, who was turned into a pillar of salt (Genesis 19:26).

ANY SIGN OF SODOM AND GOMORRAH?

The Bible records that in the days of Abraham an alliance of five cities stretched along a well-watered plain in the southern Jordan River valley (Genesis 13:10–11). At least two of these cities—Sodom and Gomorrah—were destroyed by a spectacular storm of fire and burning sulfur as an act of God's judgment (Genesis 19:24–29). Many scholars have concluded that the story of Sodom and Gomorrah is a myth or at best the exaggeration of a kernel of truth. But excavations in the 1960s and 1970s at a site on the east side of the Dead Sea (a site called Bab edh-Dhra) revealed the ruins of an extensive fortified city. What caught the attention of the excavators was a layer of ash seven feet thick—the evidence of destruction by fire! Many archaeologists have concluded that this is the site of the biblical city of Sodom.

▲ Brick making was simple but backbreaking labor. Mud from the Nile was mixed with straw and dried in the hot sun.

▲ **THE CARTOUCHE** (car-**tuush**) of Ramses—an elliptical symbol enclosing the royal name. Ramses had his name stamped on every brick used in his extensive building projects, projects made possible (perhaps) by an abundance of Hebrew slave labor!

PHARAOH HARDENED HIS HEART

The descendants of Abraham, Isaac, and Jacob grew strong during their four-hundred -year stay in Egypt—too strong. The Egyptians feared their numbers and gradually forced the Hebrews into slavery. God's people became Egypt's work force, building cities and monuments under Pharaoh's direction. Bible students have tried for decades to put the historical and biblical pieces together to discover exactly when the people of Israel left Egypt and who the Pharaoh of the Exodus really was. Two possibilities have emerged. Some scholars hold to an early date for the Exodus, around 1450 B.C. For them the hard-hearted Pharaoh of the Exodus is either Thutmose III (ruled 1485–1450 BC) or Amenhotep II (ruled 1450–1424). The early view fits best with the biblical time frame but lacks support from archaeology.

Most Old Testament scholars believe that Ramses II was the ruler who refused to let Israel go (ruled 1304–1238 BC). Their date for Israel's deliverance from Egypt is later, around 1250 BC. This later date fits with archaeological evidence but doesn't harmonize well with biblical chronology. Nothing has been found in Egyptian records that gives us a clue about the Hebrews' escape, but we would hardly expect a proud world power to write about such a humiliating defeat at the hands of a band of slaves and their foreign God!

WHICH WAY TO CANAAN?

When the Israelites left Egypt, the most direct route to Canaan would have been along the Mediterranean Sea—"the road through the Philistine country" (Exodus 13:17). God directed Moses to take the people by a much longer southern path through the wilderness. An Israeli archaeologist may have figured out why. Trude Dothan discovered a military outpost at Deir el-Balah in the Gaza Strip that was constructed during the reign of Ramses' father, Seti I. The Egyptians had built fortresses all along the northern route. God knew that his people were not prepared to face "war" with the Egyptian troops stationed in these fortresses. The Egyptian soldiers would have been eager to recapture and return these runaway slaves. God's route not only brought the people before him at Mount Sinai; it also protected them from further attack.

▼ *Egyptian soldiers*

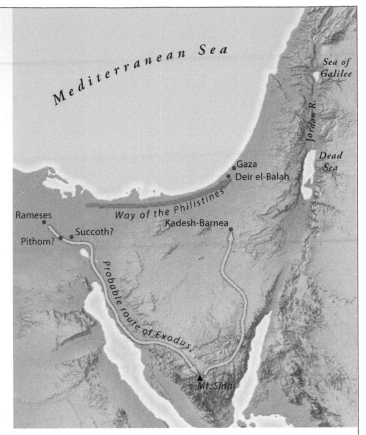

▲ *No one knows for certain the path Israel took in the wilderness but a highly likely route is shown above.*

◄ Colossal statutes of Ramses and his queen at Abu Simbel.

▼ **AMENHOTEP II** was skilled as a horseman and an athlete. One of his most celebrated feats was shooting arrows into copper targets while riding at top speed in a chariot. The reins are tied around his waist. Amenhotep made only a few campaigns into Canaan and largely ignored the region.

◄ **THUTMOSE III** has been called the Napoleon of ancient Egypt because of his extensive military campaigns and expansionist government. As the result of eighteen military initiatives into the region, Canaan became a buffer zone between Egypt and the powers to the north, particularly the Hittites. Thutmose was also an energetic builder in Egypt.

MENEPTAH'S STELE

The earliest reference to Israel as a nation outside the Bible comes from Egypt. In 1896 a large granite memorial was discovered in the funeral temple of Pharaoh Meneptah (ruled Egypt from 1224 to 1214 BC). The memorial describes his military accomplishments. What amazed Bible students was the mention of "Israel" as a people group living in Canaan. Meneptah wrote: "Israel is laid waste; his seed is not. Canaan has been plundered." Critics of the Bible claim that Israel was not a national entity until at least the time of David. This inscription provides independent evidence that Israel was recognized as early as 1200 BC as a separate people, settled in a definite place—exactly the way the Bible describes them!

▶ The hieroglyphic text above the painting tells us that this group of foreigners had come to Egypt under the leadership of their chief Absha. Perhaps they came to trade or maybe they were looking for a new place to live.

▼ "The Flight to Egypt" by He Qi, a contemporary Chinese Christian artist

OUT OF EGYPT

In a small Egyptian village known as Beni-Hasan, a nobleman named Amen-em-hat decorated his burial cave with brightly colored murals of every day life in Egypt. One scene depicts thirty-seven nomadic people from the region of Canaan in the early second millennium before Christ (about 1890 BC). We don't know exactly who these people are, of course, but we can imagine that we are looking at Abraham and Sarah and their family as they came into Egypt (Genesis 12:10) or Jacob and his sons as Joseph welcomed them into Egypt (Genesis 42:5; 43:11; 46:5–7). The mural is a window into the days of the Bible's patriarchs. The brightly colored clothes, the musical instruments, the weapons, and even the hairstyles bring the early fathers of Israel to life.

Israel and Egypt interact all the way through the Old Testament. Moses leads the people of Israel out of Egyptian slavery. Egyptian leaders try repeatedly to exercise control over the land of Israel. At the beginning of the New Testament, Jesus' parents take him to Egypt to escape Herod's attempts to murder the child. We aren't surprised then to find some remarkable discoveries that link the people of the Bible to the ancient culture of Egypt.

▲ MOSES LEADING ISRAEL ACROSS THE RED SEA The people of Israel never forgot God's mighty deliverance from Egyptian slavery.

▼ Some of the majestic pyramids had been in existence hundreds of years by the time Abraham arrived in Egypt around 2100 BC.

▲ **SOON AFTER KING SOLOMON DIED** and his kingdom split in two, the Bible says, "Sishak king of Egypt attacked Jerusalem" (1 Kings 14:25–26). The Egyptian version of that invasion, discovered carved on the walls of a temple at Karnak, tells how extensive the invasion was. More than 150 villages were looted and destroyed by the Egyptian army. Each hieroglyphic symbol represents a village in Canaan.

THE HEBREWS ARE COMING! (AMARNA LETTERS)

An Egyptian woman digging in the mounds of dirt near her home in the village of Amarna came upon lumps of hardened clay that she thought were worthless. It turned out that the small bricks of dried clay were priceless artifacts—diplomatic letters written by Babylonian and Canaanite rulers to their protector, the Egyptian Pharaoh. The letters from Canaan mention attacks from roving bands of outsiders—the *Habiru*. Were these Habiru actually the *Hebrews* under Joshua's leadership who were conquering the land God had promised to Abraham?

Some scholars believe that the four hundred Amarna letters give us exactly that—stunning, confirming evidence of Israel's successful military campaign against the Canaanite cities. Other scholars disagree, claiming that the letters date to the wrong time (1370–1335 BC)—too early for Israel's appearance in Canaan. What is clear is that the presence of nomadic people in Canaan was not unusual and Egypt seemed powerless to help. When Joshua led the people of Israel into the land, the Canaanites were in a panic!

◀ **THE AMARNA LETTERS** confirm the Bible's claim that God put great fear in the hearts of the Canaanites for the people of Israel—"our hearts melted and everyone's courage failed because of you" (Joshua 2:11).

▼ **NEFERTITI** was Pharaoh Akhenaten's queen. This stunning limestone bust of the famous queen was found at Amarna. She had six daughters with Akhenaten, two of whom became queens of Egypt.

▼ The tablets found at Amarna were not written in Egyptian hieroglyphics but in Babylonian-style cuneiform writing. No cuneiform tablets had ever been found in Egypt before this!

▲ A close-up of the cuneiform (arrow-shaped) style of writing.

◄ **AKHENATEN** (ruler of Egypt 1350–1334 BC) was more concerned with the worship of the sun god, Aten, than with the condition of the outer reaches of his empire. He was succeeded on the throne by the famous "King Tut" (Tutankhamen).

▼ **NINETY-FOUR OF THE AMARNA LETTERS** are now in the British Museum (after being smuggled out of Egypt), two hundred are in the State Museum of Berlin, and fifty stayed in Egypt. A few made their way into private collections. Below is the translation of a letter from Abdu-Heba of Jerusalem to Pharaoh Akhenaten, pleading for Egyptian help.

▼ Ancient scribes wrote and copied diplomatic letters as well as contracts and governmental decrees. The skill of writing made scribes powerful members of society and they often held positions as diplomats and political advisors.

While the king, my lord, lives, I will say to the commissioner of the king, my lord: "Why do you favor the Habiru and are opposed to the rulers?" . . . Oh king, my lord, there are no garrison troops here! May the king take care of his land!

JERICHO'S WALLS

No biblical site has attracted more attention than the city of Jericho. The Bible says that when Joshua and the people of Israel entered the promised land of Canaan, they marched around the city at God's direction and the walls collapsed (Joshua 6). If any event in the biblical story should have left evidence behind, this was certainly the one.

But we are still waiting for conclusive archaeological evidence of Jericho's fall. Scholars have argued over what has been uncovered for decades. In the 1930s John Garstang, a British explorer, stunned the world with his claims to have uncovered piles of mud bricks—the remains of the walls that fell before Joshua's armies. Twenty years later, another British scholar, Kathleen Kenyon, claimed that the remains Garstang found were actually from about 2400 BC, far too early for Joshua's conquest. She based her conclusions more on what she didn't find (pottery imported from Cyprus) rather than what she did find. Digging continues at Jericho from time to time but the best we can say at this point is that erosion and time have simply obliterated the ruins of Joshua's Jericho—until another explorer finds some new evidence that unlocks the secrets of this famous city!

▲ **THIS BRONZE PANEL** depicting Joshua and the people of Israel at Jericho was cast by Lorenzo Ghiberti in the early 15th century. It is part of a massive door and altar in Florence, Italy, called "The Gates of Paradise."

▶ **JERICHO** is one of the oldest inhabited cities in the world. Part of the appeal of the place is its location—an oasis in a desert region about ten miles northwest of the Dead Sea. Long before the people of Israel even existed, the people of Jericho fashioned plaster replicas of loved ones over the deceased person's skull!

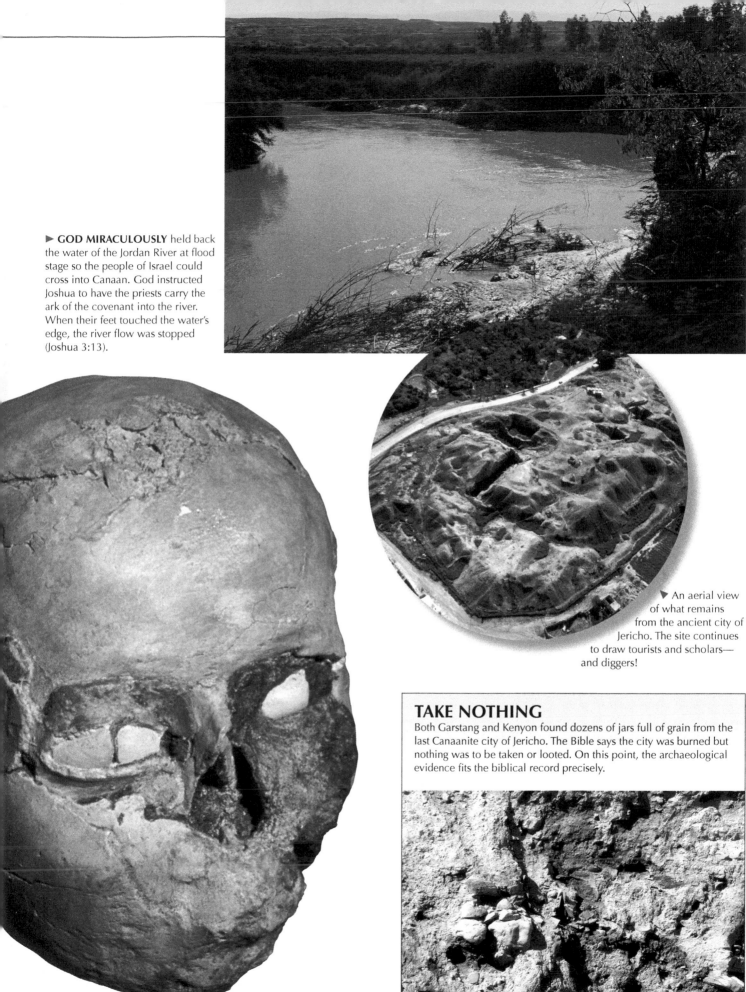

► **GOD MIRACULOUSLY** held back the water of the Jordan River at flood stage so the people of Israel could cross into Canaan. God instructed Joshua to have the priests carry the ark of the covenant into the river. When their feet touched the water's edge, the river flow was stopped (Joshua 3:13).

► An aerial view of what remains from the ancient city of Jericho. The site continues to draw tourists and scholars— and diggers!

TAKE NOTHING

Both Garstang and Kenyon found dozens of jars full of grain from the last Canaanite city of Jericho. The Bible says the city was burned but nothing was to be taken or looted. On this point, the archaeological evidence fits the biblical record precisely.

◄ The great king Solomon turned away from obedience to the Lord to follow the false gods of his foreign born wives.

NO OTHER GODS

Israel was surrounded by people who worshiped false gods. As loudly as God's prophets preached about the emptiness of abandoning the true God, God's people were often lured away from allegiance to the Lord into the idolatry and immorality of the pagan worship around them. We now know what these pagan idols looked like, and we have detailed information about what their worship involved. Excavations in the lands of the Bible have helped us get a pretty clear picture of many of the foreign deities named in Scripture. Gods and goddesses condemned by the prophets suddenly take on very real form!

◄ **DAGON WAS THE NATIONAL DEITY** of the Philistines, people who lived west of Israel along the Mediterranean coast. When the Philistines captured the ark of the covenant and placed it in the temple of Dagon, God caused the image of Dagon to tumble and break apart on the temple floor (1 Samuel 5:1–7).

◄ **ASTARTE** was the principal goddess of the Phoenicians and represented the productive power of nature. The Canaanites called her Asherah or Ashtoreth, and pictured her as the consort of Baal or even as the wife of Israel's God, Yahweh. Some Bible place names, such as Be Eshtarah (or Beth-Ashtoreth, "house of Ashtoreth"; Joshua 21:27), suggest that they were once places where the Canaanite goddess worship was centered.

◄ When Moses stayed too long on Mount Sinai, the people of Israel persuaded Aaron to craft a golden calf as the object of their worship (Exodus 32). This Vatican fresco by Raphael is titled "The Adoration of the Calf."

▼ This horned goddess from an Edomite shrine in the desert south of Israel dates from the seventh century BC.

X-RATED WORSHIP

The Canaanites believed that, each year when Mot (Death) would kill Baal and take him to the underworld, the earth would die (winter). The goddess Ashtoreth would then descend to the underworld and restore life to Baal through a sexual encounter. Life would also be restored to the earth (spring). An essential element of Canaanite worship was to re-enact this sexual encounter with cultic prostitutes in sacred groves or at worship centers called high places. God detested this perversion of worship and the prophets throughout Israel's history warned the people of God's judgment on those who practiced such immoral behavior. (For further insight read the words of Hosea in Hosea 4:12–13; 9:1–2; and 13:1.)

▲ *The Canaanites revered Reshef as the lord of battle. The Egyptians adopted Reshef as one of their gods and pictured him as the Pharaoh striking his enemies.*

Child sacrifice was a key element in the worship of Chemosh in Moab and Molech in Ammon—two of Israel's neighbors. Excavations of a pagan temple near Amman, Jordan, have revealed large numbers of human bones (many of them belonging to children) and abundant evidence of a fire cult. The prophets spoke vehemently against such sadistic and cruel practices (Isaiah 57:3–5; Jeremiah 19:3–5).

One scholar who studied the practices of the Canaanites drew this conclusion: "The amazing thing about the gods, as they were conceived in Canaan, is that they had no moral character whatsoever. In fact, their conduct was on a much lower level than that of society as a whole.... Worship of these gods carried with it some of the most demoralizing practices then in existence. Among them were child sacrifices, a practice long before discarded in Egypt and Babylonia, sacred prostitution, and snake-worship on a scale unknown among other peoples."*

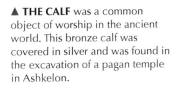

▲ **THE CALF** was a common object of worship in the ancient world. This bronze calf was covered in silver and was found in the excavation of a pagan temple in Ashkelon.

► A Canaanite worship center (or "high place") uncovered at Megiddo. Some high places (lesser sanctuaries) were devoted to the worship of the Lord, but most were places of idolatrous worship that God despised.

HUNTING FOR HITTITES

The Bible refers to the Hittites forty-seven times—but no one could find one! The Bible lists them as one of the nations living in the region of Canaan during the time of Abraham (Genesis 15:20) and says that a thousand years later they purchased horses from King Solomon (1 Kings 10:29), but critics of the Bible doubted that people called Hittites ever existed. Not one shred of historical evidence of Hittites had ever been found.

In 1876, however, a British scholar, A. H. Sayce, proposed that an unknown language found carved on building stones in Syria and Turkey might be the Hittite language. In 1906 German explorers began to search the ruins of an ancient city in Turkey called Bogazkoy. After uncovering five temples, magnificent sculptures, and over 10,000 clay tablets, they announced to the world that the Hittites had been found! Not only was the historical reliability of the Bible confirmed again, but also scholars were able to fill in the political and cultural landscape of the Old Testament much more accurately with the art, history, and military exploits of Israel's neighbor to the north.

▼ **BORGAZKOY** (also called Hattusha) was the capital of an extensive Hittite empire that reached the height of its power from 1400 to 1200 BC. These stone lions at the city gates stood with their mouths open in order to ward off evil spirits and intimidate visiting dignitaries.

▶ **TWO HITTITES STAND OUT** prominently in the Old Testament story: Ephron, the Hittite who sold a cave to Abraham as a burial place for Sarah (Genesis 23:10–20)—a place traditionally located in Hebron and called the tomb of the Patriarchs; and Uriah the Hittite, the loyal servant of David and the husband of Bathsheba (2 Samuel 10–11). The medieval manuscript illustration (right) shows Uriah receiving the letter from King David that ordered Uriah's death.

▶ A sculpture of a Hittite soldier. While the Hittite empire maintained a large and well-equipped army, Hittite law codes preferred diplomacy, when possible, to military force. Conquered enemies were treated with clemency rather than torture or execution.

▲ **EVEN AFTER THE COLLAPSE OF THE HITTITE EMPIRE** around 1200 BC, the people in the same region who traced their lineage to the Hittites or who continued to speak the Hittite language were called Hittites. Small city kingdoms of Hittites existed into the eighth century BC, the date of this sculpture of a royal prince in his nurse's arms. The Assyrians and Babylonians continued to refer to the region as "the land of the Hittites" hundreds of years after the Hittites were overcome by peoples from their western border.

HITTITE TREATIES AND GOD'S COVENANTS

Among the tablets discovered in the ruins of the Hittite capital were two dozen treaty documents, including this treaty between Ramses II of Egypt and Muwatallish of the Hittites. The Kadesh Treaty (named after the city where it was drawn up) is the first known written treaty between nations. A study of Hittite treaties has shed significant light on the covenants of the Old Testament made between God and his people Israel. The cultural form of a political treaty provided a convenient and well-understood format for a spiritual covenant. Many of the elements found in Hittite treaties (blessings on those who keep the treaty and curses on those who don't, for example) found their way into biblical covenants. The Hittite treaty formulas also verify that our biblical documents were written early in Israel's history, not hundreds of years later as some critics contend.

◀ **THE ARAMAIC INSCRIPTION** on black basalt was found at the northern Israelite site of Tel Dan. The phrase "house of David" is highlighted in the photo. The reconstructed inscription reads: "I killed Jehoram son of Ahab king of Israel and I killed Ahaziah son of Jehoram king of the house of David." The Aramaeans to Israel's northeast were subdued by David but, as the nation of Israel divided and weakened after David's death, Aram regained its independence and power.

Excavations at Dan have uncovered the ninth century BC foundations of the gate of the city where the king sat in judgment over the people. This photo shows a partial reconstruction of the gate area. ▼

MYTHIC KING OR MAN OF GOD?

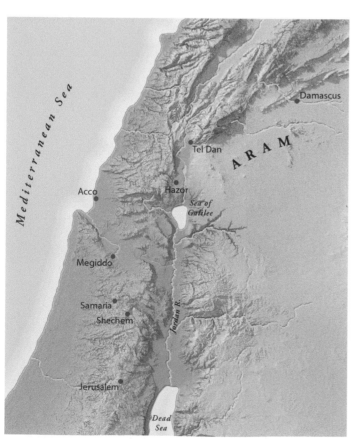

Critics of the Bible have contended for a long time that David was not a real person. He was (they claim) just a mythic character created to show Israel what a "good" king was like. The critics based their doubts about David on the fact that no record of David has been found outside the Bible. But in 1993 that all changed.

A stone slab was discovered in the most northern region of Old Testament Israel. The inscription on the slab exalted the deeds of a king of Aram, the nation to the north and east of ancient Israel. The man who discovered the inscription, Avraham Biran, believes that the Aramean king was Hazael, a ruler mentioned several times in the Bible. What makes the inscription so astonishing is its reference to "the house of David." If there was a "house of David," that is, a ruling family descended from David, then there must have been a real man with that name. The critics had to go back to the drawing board—again.

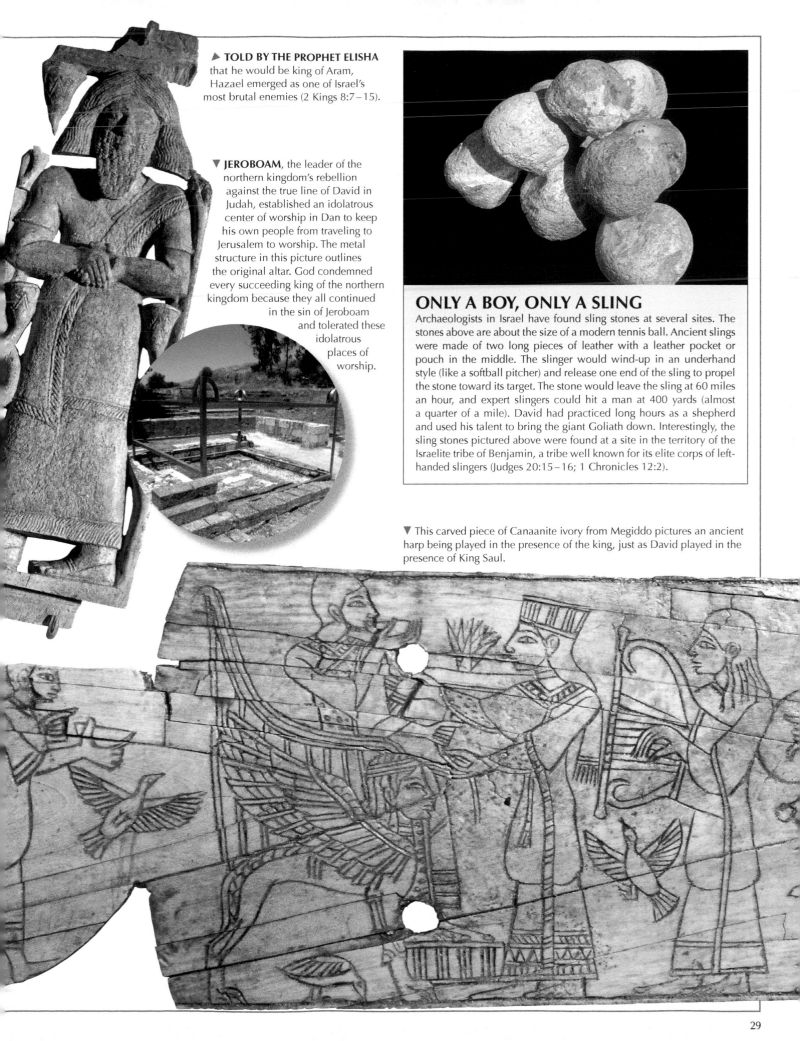

▶ **TOLD BY THE PROPHET ELISHA** that he would be king of Aram, Hazael emerged as one of Israel's most brutal enemies (2 Kings 8:7–15).

▼ **JEROBOAM**, the leader of the northern kingdom's rebellion against the true line of David in Judah, established an idolatrous center of worship in Dan to keep his own people from traveling to Jerusalem to worship. The metal structure in this picture outlines the original altar. God condemned every succeeding king of the northern kingdom because they all continued in the sin of Jeroboam and tolerated these idolatrous places of worship.

ONLY A BOY, ONLY A SLING

Archaeologists in Israel have found sling stones at several sites. The stones above are about the size of a modern tennis ball. Ancient slings were made of two long pieces of leather with a leather pocket or pouch in the middle. The slinger would wind-up in an underhand style (like a softball pitcher) and release one end of the sling to propel the stone toward its target. The stone would leave the sling at 60 miles an hour, and expert slingers could hit a man at 400 yards (almost a quarter of a mile). David had practiced long hours as a shepherd and used his talent to bring the giant Goliath down. Interestingly, the sling stones pictured above were found at a site in the territory of the Israelite tribe of Benjamin, a tribe well known for its elite corps of left-handed slingers (Judges 20:15–16; 1 Chronicles 12:2).

▼ This carved piece of Canaanite ivory from Megiddo pictures an ancient harp being played in the presence of the king, just as David played in the presence of King Saul.

▲ The Philistines were well-known in the ancient world for their distinctive and highly decorative pottery.

◄ A stunning Philistine dagger found in Ekron.

◄ **THE GIANT GOLIATH** was the champion of the Philistine army—and was killed by a shepherd boy!

FINDING THE PHILISTINES

The Philistines were one of Israel's fiercest enemies. During the days of the judges and the kingdom of Saul and David, the Philistines were a constant source of attack and aggravation. Two of the best known biblical Philistines tried to destroy the people of Israel—Delilah and Goliath!

Ekron was one of the major Philistine cities, but it had never been found. (You will find Ekron mentioned in the Bible in Joshua 13:3 and in twenty-three other places.) In the 1980s, an Israeli and an American worked to uncover an ancient mound that they were certain contained the buried city of Ekron. Their hunch paid off! The most remarkable find in the city was a stone inscription that not only positively identified the city but named five of its kings—two of whom are mentioned in the Bible. The discoveries at Ekron fill in important details about these people who gave Israel so much grief.

▼ This stone commemorated the dedication of a huge temple complex in Ekron. The king at the time (around 690 BC) was Achish, son of Padi. The inscription itself contains five lines of seventy-one letters.

▲ Samson destroyed himself and thousands of Philistines in his final act of judgment on these enemies of Israel. It would be much later, under David's reign, that the Philistines would finally be subdued.

▼ ONE OF THE BEST PORTRAITS OF THE PHILISTINES comes from carvings celebrating Egypt's defeat of the Philistine invasion around 1250 BC. The Philistines are marked out by their feathered headdresses.

▲ The Philistines buried their dead in coffins carved or molded into human likenesses.

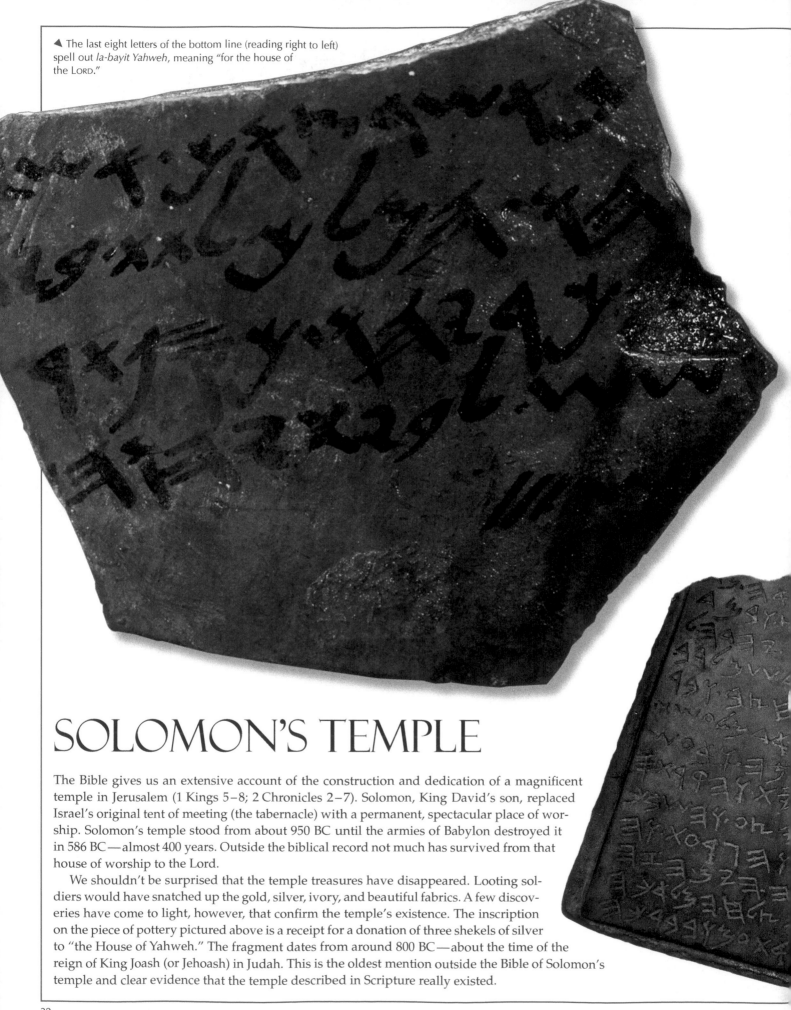

◄ The last eight letters of the bottom line (reading right to left) spell out *la-bayit Yahweh*, meaning "for the house of the LORD."

SOLOMON'S TEMPLE

The Bible gives us an extensive account of the construction and dedication of a magnificent temple in Jerusalem (1 Kings 5–8; 2 Chronicles 2–7). Solomon, King David's son, replaced Israel's original tent of meeting (the tabernacle) with a permanent, spectacular place of worship. Solomon's temple stood from about 950 BC until the armies of Babylon destroyed it in 586 BC—almost 400 years. Outside the biblical record not much has survived from that house of worship to the Lord.

We shouldn't be surprised that the temple treasures have disappeared. Looting soldiers would have snatched up the gold, silver, ivory, and beautiful fabrics. A few discoveries have come to light, however, that confirm the temple's existence. The inscription on the piece of pottery pictured above is a receipt for a donation of three shekels of silver to "the House of Yahweh." The fragment dates from around 800 BC—about the time of the reign of King Joash (or Jehoash) in Judah. This is the oldest mention outside the Bible of Solomon's temple and clear evidence that the temple described in Scripture really existed.

GOD'S HOLY NAME

The Lord's name in Hebrew is written with four letters—yhwh—and is pronounced "Yahweh." Modern English versions translate the name as "the LORD." The word pictured above is the divine name as it appears in the Leningrad Codex; it is pictured below as it appears in a modern printed Hebrew Bible. Hebrew is read from right to left, the opposite of English.

יְהוָה

▲ **THIS INSCRIBED PIECE OF POTTERY** (called an ostracon) was found at the ancient city of Arad and dates from the early 6th century BC. It is a letter that mentions "the House of Yahweh" in Jerusalem—another reference outside the Bible to the original temple.

◀ **DIGGERS AT THE CITY** of Arad also uncovered a 10th century BC temple that was modeled after Solomon's temple in Jerusalem with courtyards, a holy place, and a holy of holies—the inner room where God's presence rested. Such alternate temples and "high places" were tolerated by some of Judah's kings until the time of Hezekiah, who returned the worship of the Lord to the place God had ordained (2 Kings 18:4). Two incense altars were found in the Arad temple. They were laying on their side and were covered with dirt, perhaps to protect them after the temple was "closed."

▶ Solomon dedicates the temple to the Lord. God displayed his acceptance of the new worship center by filling the temple sanctuary with the brilliant light of his glory (2 Chronicles 7:1–3).

◀ **IN 2003 AN INSCRIBED TABLET** came to light that appeared to be written at the same time as the temple receipt and during the reign of the same King Jehoash, a ninth century BC ruler of Judah. It describes the collection of money for the repair of the temple in Jerusalem (2 Kings 12:5–17). In late 2004 the document was declared to be a forgery and the antiquities dealer who sold it was indicted in Israel.

▲ **THIS MODEL OF THE ARK** shows the figures of angels with outstretched wings protecting the place of mercy, the solid gold lid where Israel's high priest sprinkled blood for the atonement of sins.

THE LOST ARK

The most revered piece of furniture in the original tabernacle and later in Solomon's temple was the ark of the covenant. The ark disappeared after the destruction of the temple by the Babylonian army in 586 BC, and no one has been able to find it. Two discoveries, however, have brought us closer to the actual ark.

The first discovery was made in Egypt in 1922. A British explorer, Howard Carter, cut a hole through a sealed doorway and discovered the tomb of Pharaoh Tutankhamun—untouched since the fourteenth century BC. Among the treasures was a magnificent wooden chest, probably designed to carry the Pharaoh's royal robes. Four poles were used to carry the box, two at each end. The poles were stored by sliding them through rings underneath the chest—almost exactly the way the ark of the covenant was carried.

The second discovery was made as scholars closely studied the area where the original temple stood—an area now inside the Muslim shrine called the Dome of the Rock and off-limits to non-Muslims. In the center of where the innermost room of the temple would have been (called the Holy of Holies in the Bible) is a rectangular depression carved in the precise dimensions of the ark of the covenant. This flat spot marked the exact place where the ark sat during the days of Solomon's temple.

WILL THE TEMPLE BE REBUILT?

Ultra-conservative Jews in Israel believe that when the Messiah comes, Israel's temple worship will be restored. They have already begun to prepare vessels and priestly garments for that future day. Many Christians believe that the temple will be rebuilt during the days of the future Tribulation. The main obstacle to a rebuilt temple is the presence of the Muslim holy places on the platform where the temple once stood. Only God knows how such an impasse will be overcome.

▶ David dancing before the ark of the covenant—an illustration from the Breviary of Martin of Aragon, 15th century Spain. David brought the ark to the city of Jerusalem, but it was David's son, Solomon, who built the temple as a permanent sanctuary in Israel.

▲ Some scholars believe that a depression in the "foundation stone" is the place where the ark rested. Muslims revere the same spot as the place from which the prophet Muhammad took a midnight ride into heaven.

◀ **MONKS IN THE ETHIOPIAN ORTHODOX CHURCH** claim to possess the original ark, stolen for safekeeping from the temple at the time of Solomon's death. The Bible refers to the ark more than two hundred times up until the end of Solomon's reign and almost never after that. No proof beyond their claim has ever been provided to the rest of the world.

▶ **A WOODEN BOX FROM TUTANKHAMEN'S TOMB** similar to the ark, the holy chest that held the stone tablets of Israel's law. The dog-god stands guard over the contents of the box much like the cherubs "guarded" the ark of the covenant.

SOLOMON'S CITIES

The temple wasn't Solomon's only building project. In order to protect the trade route that ran through Israel from Egypt to Damascus, Solomon rebuilt or fortified the strategic cities of Hazor, Megiddo and Gezer (1 Kings 9:15). Explorers have found the very gates and fortresses that Solomon supervised. Solomon also expanded the technology of warfare. His father, David, had refused to use chariots, but Solomon saw them as the next stage of military effectiveness. He stationed chariot divisions throughout his kingdom and especially in the cities any enemy would attack first. Several stable/storehouse structures from Solomon's day have been discovered and partially reconstructed.

▼ This 13th-century illustration shows David sitting in judgment of the people at the gates of Jerusalem.

► **LARGE, VAULTED AREAS** underneath the temple platform in Jerusalem were mistakenly called Solomon's Stables by Christian crusaders in the middle ages. The structures were actually built during Herod's expansion of the temple courtyard 900 years after Solomon's death. The height of the room is about 30 feet. The Crusaders used the area for stabling animals.

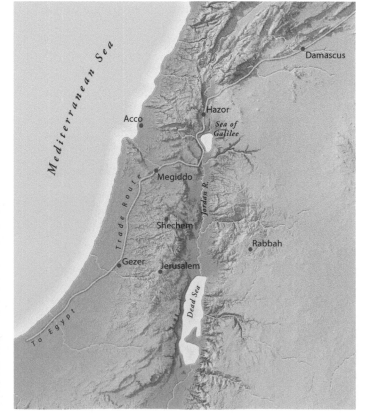

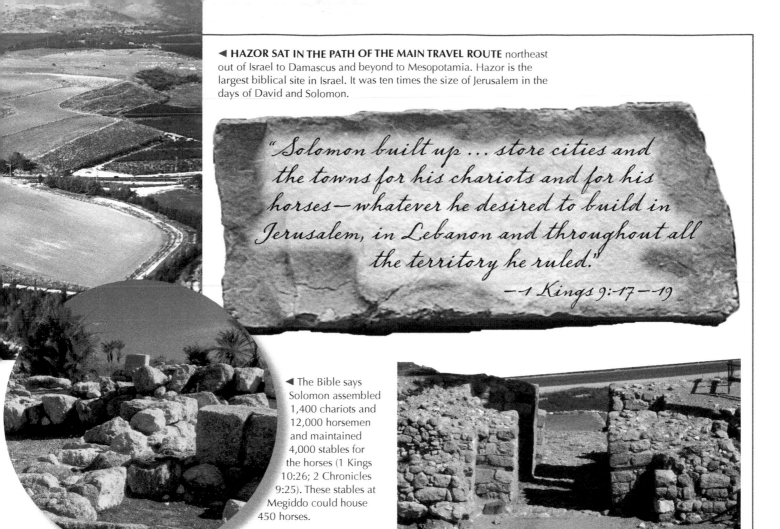

◄ **HAZOR SAT IN THE PATH OF THE MAIN TRAVEL ROUTE** northeast out of Israel to Damascus and beyond to Mesopotamia. Hazor is the largest biblical site in Israel. It was ten times the size of Jerusalem in the days of David and Solomon.

"Solomon built up ... store cities and the towns for his chariots and for his horses—whatever he desired to build in Jerusalem, in Lebanon and throughout all the territory he ruled."

—*1 Kings 9:17 – 19*

◄ The Bible says Solomon assembled 1,400 chariots and 12,000 horsemen and maintained 4,000 stables for the horses (1 Kings 10:26; 2 Chronicles 9:25). These stables at Megiddo could house 450 horses.

SITTING IN THE CITY GATES

The fortified gates at Megiddo and Gezer were made up of a series of rooms, each lined with plastered benches where the city's business was transacted. You can almost see Boaz negotiating for the privilege of marrying Ruth before the elders of the city (Ruth 4:1) or Lot sitting in the gate of Sodom (Genesis 19:1) or Absalom, David's son, standing outside the gates and passing judgment on the people's complaints (2 Samuel 15:2 – 4). In wartime, armed troops could hide in the rooms, waiting to neutralize any enemy troops who tried to enter the city.

◄ **SOLOMON IMPORTED CHARIOT WARFARE** from the stronger political powers of the region, like the Assyrians and the Egyptians. An Assyrian chariot is pictured here. Chariot warfare was difficult in the hilly terrain of central Israel around Jerusalem but chariots were very effective on the more level ground of the trade routes.

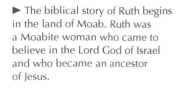

► The biblical story of Ruth begins in the land of Moab. Ruth was a Moabite woman who came to believe in the Lord God of Israel and who became an ancestor of Jesus.

◄ The land of Moab was largely wilderness, suited primarily for raising sheep and goats that could be moved from place to place in search of grass.

▲ The artwork above pictures Ruth gleaning in the fields of Israel to provide food for herself and her mother-in-law, Naomi. Boaz, the field's owner, would become her husband.

◄ **ANOTHER MOABITE INSCRIPTION** This inscription is one of the few examples of the Moabite language that has survived. A construction crew digging a trench at a building site found the piece in Jordan near the town of El-Kerak in 1958. It was probably part of a larger monument, perhaps a statue, and it dates from about the same time as the Moabite Stone (9th century BC).

THE MOABITE STONE

"I am Mesha, son of Chemosh, king of Moab"—those are the opening words of one of the most remarkable biblical discoveries ever found. Mesha was the ruler of Moab, a tribal kingdom east of the Dead Sea. In the middle of the ninth century BC, Moab languished under the domination of the northern kingdom of Israel. King Omri and his son, Ahab, laid a heavy tax burden on Moab. When weaker kings came to the throne, Mesha saw his chance to rebel and throw off the shackles of foreign oppression. He pushed Israel out, won back his territory, and rebuilt some of his towns. He was so proud of his accomplishments that he had the whole story carved in stone and erected in his fortress at Dibon.

When scholars tried to buy this stone monument in the late 1860s, local residents thought there had to be some kind of treasure inside. The writing meant nothing to them. So they heated the stone over an outdoor fire and then poured cold water on it. The stone shattered (as expected) but no treasure was found. One French discoverer tried to collect all the pieces but only recovered about three-fifths of the original inscription. Fortunately, copies and an impression of the stone had been made before it was destroyed. The Moabite Stone (or Mesha Stone) is the only monument to survive from Moab, Israel's neighbor. It is the longest inscription on a monument yet discovered in the Holy Land.

WELL-KNOWN IN THE WORLD; UNKNOWN TO GOD

Remains of Omri's palace in Samaria. King Omri gets only a few verses in the biblical text, but he was well known and widely respected in the political world of his day. Phrases like "the land of Omri" and "the house of Omri" have been found in the texts of the Assyrian empire in reference to Israel. In God's eyes, however, Omri was the wickedest of Israel's kings and deserved only passing reference.

▶ **THE INSCRIPTION** is written using old Phoenician letters in a language very similar to early Hebrew. Mesha's original black basalt monument was 3 feet, 9 inches high and 27 inches wide at the base. 669 of the estimated 1,100 letters of the original inscription were recovered after the stone was broken. The Berlin Museum negotiated for the monument but the French Consulate in Jerusalem offered more money. The stone resides today in the Louvre in Paris.

◀ **MESHA DEDICATED THE STONE MONUMENT TO CHEMOSH,** the national god of Moab. He believed that Chemosh had "delivered me from all kings" and had given him "victory over all my enemies."

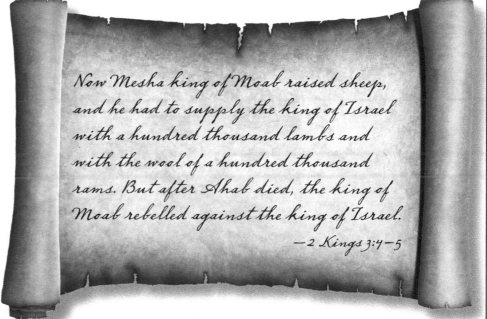

Now Mesha king of Moab raised sheep, and he had to supply the king of Israel with a hundred thousand lambs and with the wool of a hundred thousand rams. But after Ahab died, the king of Moab rebelled against the king of Israel.

—2 Kings 3:4–5

A BURIED CITY

A Syrian farmer plowing his field thought he just hit a big stone. But when he pushed it out of the way, he uncovered a passage to a forgotten city. Eventually the ancient city of Ugarit was unearthed—a city that flourished during the days of Joshua's conquest of the land of Canaan and the early period of the judges in Israel.

Among the treasures of the city and royal palace were hundreds of clay tablets covered with pointed cuneiform script. Some were written in Babylonian; others in an unknown language later called Ugaritic. More than 1500 Ugaritic tablets have been found—treaties, execution orders, and boring government documents. The most astonishing texts were the myths and legends of the Canaanites. The Bible's references to Baal and Ashtoreth suddenly took on new meaning. These discoveries at Ugarit have opened the door to the beliefs and culture of the people who lived right next door to the Old Testament Israelites. You never know what one big rock might uncover.

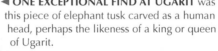

◄ **ONE EXCEPTIONAL FIND AT UGARIT** was this piece of elephant tusk carved as a human head, perhaps the likeness of a king or queen of Ugarit.

◄ **ELIJAH CHALLENGED KING AHAB AND THE PRIESTS OF BAAL** to a contest they couldn't resist. The true God would send a bolt of lightning to consume an animal sacrifice (1 Kings 18). That shouldn't have been a problem for the god of the storm—and it wasn't for the true God! David in the Psalms had often pictured the Lord shooting the arrows of lightning against his enemies (Psalm 18:14; 144:6).

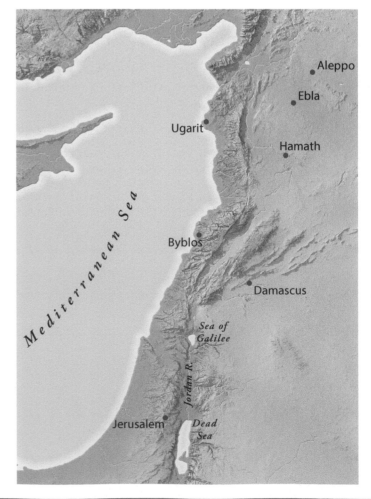

Aleppo

Ebla

Ugarit

Hamath

Byblos

Damascus

Mediterranean Sea

Sea of Galilee

Jordan R.

Jerusalem

Dead Sea

◀ Excavations at Ugarit (modern name, Ras Shamra).

▶ **BAAL IS THE CANAANITE GOD OF RAIN** and the storm, often pictured with a lightning bolt in his hand. More than 500 references to Baal have been found in Ugaritic texts.

◀ **THIS METAL IMAGE OF THE GOD, EL,** was found in Ugarit. El was worshiped as the supreme god, the creator of the world, and the father of Baal.

▶ Baal's consort is called Asherah, a fertility goddess represented by an image or, at times, by a carved pole or even a tree. Other forms of the goddess's name are: Asherim, Asheroth, and Ashtoreth. Some scholars believe there are two (or more) goddesses in Canaanite mythology; others believe that all these names refer to the same deity.

THE WORLD'S FIRST ALPHABET

The scholars deciphering Ugaritic were amazed to discover that the language was alphabetic—each symbol represented a single sound. The symbols were then combined in different ways to spell out words (just like the English language works). Other early languages (like Egyptian and Babylonian) were pictographic—one symbol stood for one word, resulting in a difficult written language made up of thousands of symbols.

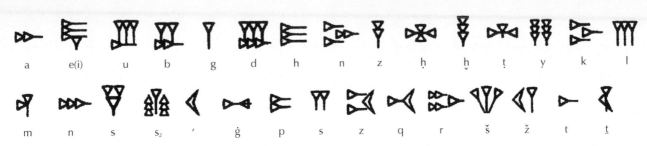

a   e(i)   u   b   g   d   h   n   z   ḥ   ḫ   ṭ   y   k   l

m   n   s   s₂   ʾ   ġ   p   ṣ   z   q   r   š   ž   t   ṯ

► **THE IMPRESSION LEFT IN CLAY** (the lumps are called bullae, or singular bulla) usually contained the person's name and a simple or elaborate design. The higher the person's rank, the more intricate and harder to counterfeit the seal became.

► **THIS CLAY SEAL BEARS THE IMPRINT OF BARUCH,** secretary and friend to Jeremiah the prophet (Jeremiah 32:12; 45:1–5). Another clay impression of Baruch's seal owned by a private collector bears a clear fingerprint along the edge—perhaps the fingerprint of an actual person mentioned in the Old Testament! Jeremiah dictated his prophecies to Baruch who not only wrote them down but read them to the people.

AUTHORIZED ACCESS ONLY

Security and privacy are not just modern problems. They caused headaches in the biblical world too. Royal messages and sensitive documents had to be protected from prying eyes. To prevent unauthorized access, the document was folded or rolled, tied with a string, and then a lump of clay or hot wax was placed on the knot. The writer's official seal was pressed into the soft clay or warm wax so everyone would know the person they would answer to if the seal was broken. Several seals or clay impressions have been discovered that relate directly or indirectly to people in the Bible.

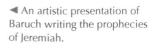

◄ An artistic presentation of Baruch writing the prophecies of Jeremiah.

A SEALED SCROLL

The most famous sealed document in the Bible is the scroll in Revelation 4 and 5 that is sealed with seven seals. Only Jesus is worthy to open that scroll. The scroll was probably not sealed seven times along the outside flap. More likely, when the writing on the scroll was completed, a section of the scroll was rolled up and sealed, then more rolled up and sealed, and so on. As each seal is broken in Revelation 6 and 7, that part of the scroll is opened and the events emerge from the exposed columns of the scroll. The apostle John watches the future spring to life as Jesus opens each section of the scroll.

▶ This scroll, found in Egypt, shows how ancient documents were sealed.

▲ A WINGED SCARAB (beetle) formed the design on the seal of Hezekiah, king of Judah. Scarab seals were particularly popular in Egypt where the dung beetle was a sacred symbol. The seal was usually worn around the neck or embedded in a ring.

THE CITY NO ONE COULD FIND

▲ **THE GOVERNMENT OF IRAQ** has reconstructed some of the walls of ancient Nineveh to attract tourists and scholars.

The city of Nineveh pops up repeatedly in the Bible. We read about it first in Genesis 10:11—"From that land [Nimrod] went to Assyria, where he built Nineveh." The next time we read about Nineveh is in the book of Jonah when the prophet is sent to preach to that "very important city" (Jonah 3:3; 2 Kings 19:36; Isaiah 37:37). The prophets Nahum and Zephaniah predicted the ruin and desolation of Nineveh as judgment from God.

The problem for centuries was that no one could find Nineveh! Its destruction was so complete that the city could no longer be located. Critics of the Bible said that Nineveh never really existed. It was just part of the mythical story of Jonah and the great fish. Serious explorers found several key cities of the Assyrian Empire, but no one could find Nineveh—until an intrepid British explorer named Henry Layard came on the scene. After several dead-end attempts, Layard uncovered the ruins of the great city of Nineveh. Magnificent palaces, huge sculptures, and astonishing libraries of clay tablets opened our understanding of the mighty power of the Assyrians—and silenced the skeptics who said Nineveh never existed.

▲ **CUNEIFORM TABLET** detailing the destruction of Nineveh in 612 BC by the Babylonian armies—exactly the way the biblical prophets said God's judgment would come!

◄ **THE MYTHICAL FIGURE OF A WINGED BULL** guarded the entrances to the royal palace. The figure represents intelligence (the reigning king's face), strength (a bull's body), and swift justice on enemies (eagle's wings).

◄ **SOLDIERS OF THE ASSYRIAN ROYAL GUARD** as depicted on a stone panel in the palace of Sennacherib.

▼ **A DYING LION** captured in stone at Nineveh.

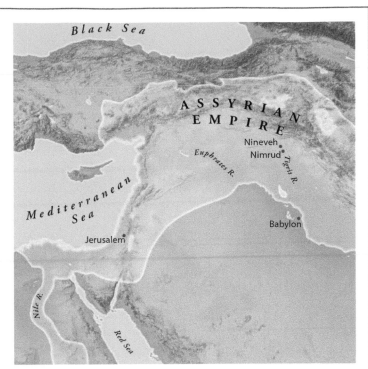

▲ The Assyrian Empire stretched from modern Iran in the east to Egypt and modern Turkey in the west.

► Hunting hounds from a sculpture in the palace of Ashurbanipal in Nineveh. Assyrian kings had their palaces adorned not only with pictures of warfare and conquest but also with scenes from every day life.

▲ **THIS OPENING ILLUSTRATION FROM THE BOOK OF NAHUM** in the "Great Bible" shows the prophet predicting the downfall of Nineveh and the powerful Assyrian empire.

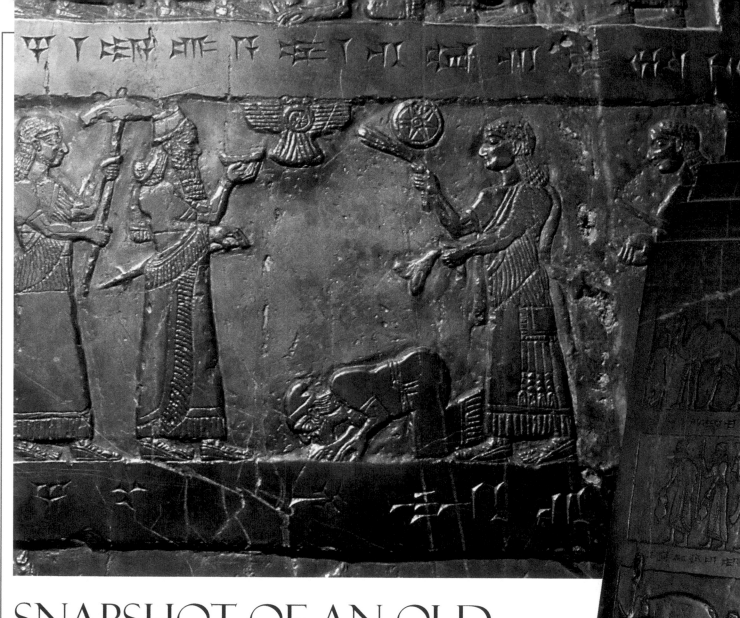

SNAPSHOT OF AN OLD TESTAMENT KING

▲ **SHALMANESER III** left more royal inscriptions and annals behind than any other Assyrian king. He didn't want to be forgotten!

One of the most exciting discoveries ever made in the lands of the Bible was a large black stone found in the ruins of the Assyrian city of Calah (modern Nimrud) in 1846. The stone was a four-sided monument (an obelisk) about six and a half feet high. The scenes carved on each side pictured rulers from all over the Assyrian empire bringing tribute to the king. More than 200 lines of cuneiform text explain the military triumphs of Shalmaneser III, who ruled Assyria from 858 to 824 BC. One carved picture stopped Old Testament scholars in their tracks! The caption read: "Tribute of Jehu, son of Omri."

The figure bowing before the Assyrian emperor was either an emissary from Jehu or Jehu himself—a biblical king snapped in a stone photograph. Jehu was the ruler of the northern kingdom of Israel during the time of Assyria's expansion westward (841–814 BC). Jehu may have paid tribute to Assyria as a direct political payout to buy Assyrian authority for his kingship. Jehu, it seems, had brutally killed king Jehoram in order to gain access to Israel's throne.

◄ King Jehu bows to the earth in submission to Shamaneser III. King Jehu was not a "son of Omri" as he is called in the inscription but, in the eyes of the Assyrians, any ruler of Israel was connected back to Israel's most illustrious king.

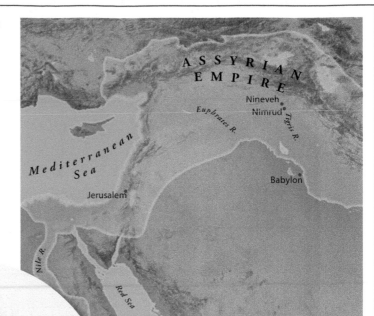

► **SHALMANESER'S MONUMENT** catalogues 31 different military campaigns. Five scenes were carved on each side, twenty in all. It was erected in 825 BC at a time of civil war in Assyria. The original stands today in the British Museum.

◄ **THE BRITISH EXPLORER HENRY LAYARD** had told his workers that he was closing down the dig. The winter ground was cold and hard, and they had found very little in their excavation. He asked his men to work just one more day—and on that day one of the most important Assyrian artifacts was found—Shalmaneser's Black Obelisk.

▼ The portraits of Jehu's servants on the Black Obelisk provide us with the earliest depictions of ordinary ancient Israelites.

WAR WITH ASSYRIA

When explorers began digging through the remains of the city of Nineveh, they found an astonishing series of thirteen carved panels that picture the attack by the armies of Assyria on the city of Lachish in Judah. The panels are the closest thing the Assyrians had to a motion picture! As you walk along the 90 foot mural, you can see the Assyrian camp, their siege and conquest of the city, the torture of some of the city's inhabitants, and the presentation of the survivors to the victorious Assyrian king. The caption under the mural claims that King Sennacherib's armies descended on Judah "like the wolf on the fold."

Sennacherib would have preferred to depict the fall of Jerusalem on his mural, but God's intervention protected Jerusalem from destruction. An angel of God swept through the enemy camp and killed 185,000 men.

In the fourteenth year of King Hezekiah's reign, Sennacherib king of Assyria attacked all the fortified cities of Judah and captured them.

—2 Kings 18:13

▲ **THE GREAT ARTIST PETER PAUL RUBENS** captured his vision of God's angel sweeping through the Assyrian camp.

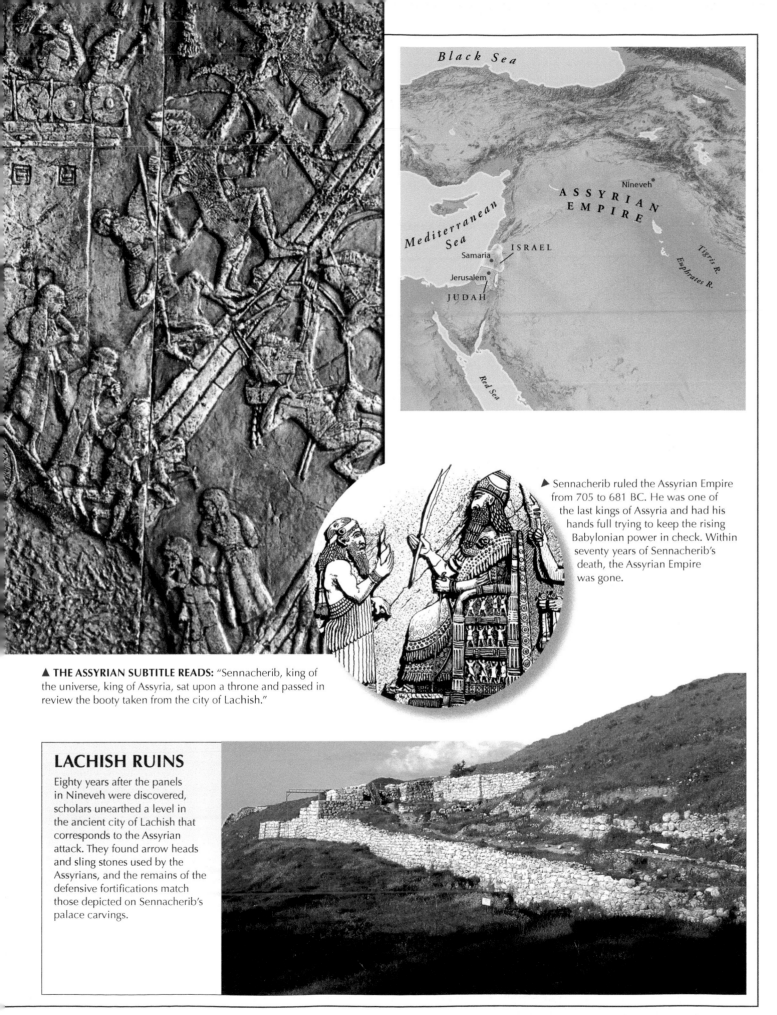

▲ THE ASSYRIAN SUBTITLE READS: "Sennacherib, king of the universe, king of Assyria, sat upon a throne and passed in review the booty taken from the city of Lachish."

▶ Sennacherib ruled the Assyrian Empire from 705 to 681 BC. He was one of the last kings of Assyria and had his hands full trying to keep the rising Babylonian power in check. Within seventy years of Sennacherib's death, the Assyrian Empire was gone.

LACHISH RUINS

Eighty years after the panels in Nineveh were discovered, scholars unearthed a level in the ancient city of Lachish that corresponds to the Assyrian attack. They found arrow heads and sling stones used by the Assyrians, and the remains of the defensive fortifications match those depicted on Sennacherib's palace carvings.

NORTHERN KINGDOM DESTROYED

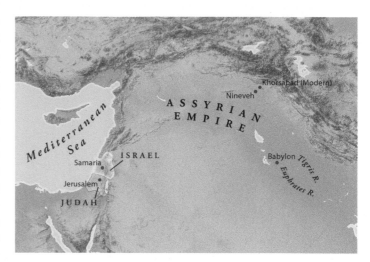

▲ A portrait of the Assyrian king, Sargon II, from his palace at Khorsabad discovered by the French explorer, Paul Botta, in 1843.

One of the earliest discoveries to interlock the Bible and ancient historical documents was found inside a spectacular palace built by Assyria's Sargon II (ruled from 722 to 705 BC). The walls of the palace were covered with accounts that celebrated the king's military victories. The account that excited Bible students most was the record of the fall of the northern kingdom of Israel to the Assyrian armies in 722 BC. For 2500 years the only known account of the siege and conquest of Israel's capital city of Samaria was found in the Bible. Now a secular historical record (the *Time* magazine of the ancient world) paralleled exactly what the Bible said.

This kind of identical battlefield reporting from both sides was very unusual. Normally the conquered nation tried to spin a defeat to sound like a victory—or they left it out of their history books altogether! But God saw to it that both the conqueror and the conquered recorded his judgment on his wayward people.

◀ One volume of the annals of Sargon.

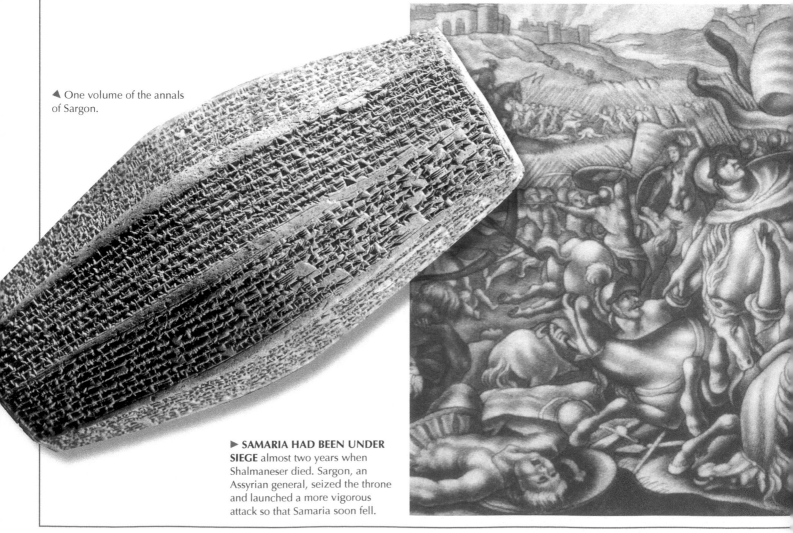

▶ SAMARIA HAD BEEN UNDER SIEGE almost two years when Shalmaneser died. Sargon, an Assyrian general, seized the throne and launched a more vigorous attack so that Samaria soon fell.

◄ A BIBLICAL MYSTERY SOLVED
The Sargon inscription also cleared up a biblical mystery. Until then, the king that conquered Samaria was thought to have been Shalmaneser V, Sargon's predecessor. Shalmaneser is mentioned in 2 Kings 17:3, but the king who took Samaria is not named. The Sargon inscription filled the gap in the biblical record.

ROYAL TOMBS OF NIMRUD
In 1989, just before the first Gulf War, Iraqi archaeologists made a startling discovery. They found intact tombs of three Assyrian queens whose names were unknown before that time—Yaba, queen to Tiglathpilesar III; Banitu, queen to Shalmaneser V; and Atalia, queen to Sargon II. The crystal objects pictured here were inscribed with queen Banitu's name.

► ENORMOUS WINGED BULLS
guarded the main doorway to Sargon's palace in Khorsabad. When the discoverer, Paul Botta, found them, he had workmen load them on rafts, float them down the Tigris River, and ship them off to Paris. You can see them today in the Louvre.

▲ THE TUNNEL runs from the water spring of Gihon to the pool of Siloam inside the old city walls. The spring was then sealed to keep enemies from gaining access to the water.

HEZEKIAH'S TUNNEL

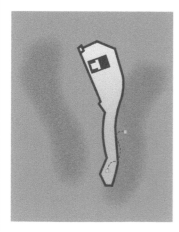

▲ Edward Robinson, an American explorer, made the first accurate survey of the tunnel in 1838—534 meters (1,750 feet) in length.

The pool of water and the dark tunnel were well-known landmarks in Jerusalem. One day in 1880 a brave boy held a candle above his head and walked into the tunnel farther than any of his friends had ever gone. To his surprise, he found words scratched on the tunnel wall. Later, six lines of Hebrew writing were recovered. The inscription told the incredible story of how two teams of workers had cut a tunnel through the rock to bring water inside the city walls. They started at opposite ends and eventually, by following the sounds of hammers and chisels, they met in the middle.

The Judean king, Hezekiah, had built just this kind of tunnel to ensure a supply of fresh water inside the city during a time of attack and siege from the Assyrian army (2 Kings 20:20; 2 Chronicles 32:3–4, 30). The reliable water source allowed the people of Jerusalem to hold out against any surrounding army.

In 1890 a Greek antiquities dealer chopped the inscription from the tunnel wall and broke it. The Turkish authorities who ruled Jerusalem at the time confiscated the inscription, and it is now on exhibit in a museum in Istanbul.

The pool of Siloam is referred to in the New Testament in John 9:7 as the place where Jesus healed a man who had been born blind. The pool and Hezekiah's Tunnel are popular tourist sites in modern Jerusalem.

▶ THE STYLE OF THE HEBREW LETTERS in what is today called the Siloam Inscription reflect perfectly the style of writing prevalent during Hezekiah's reign.

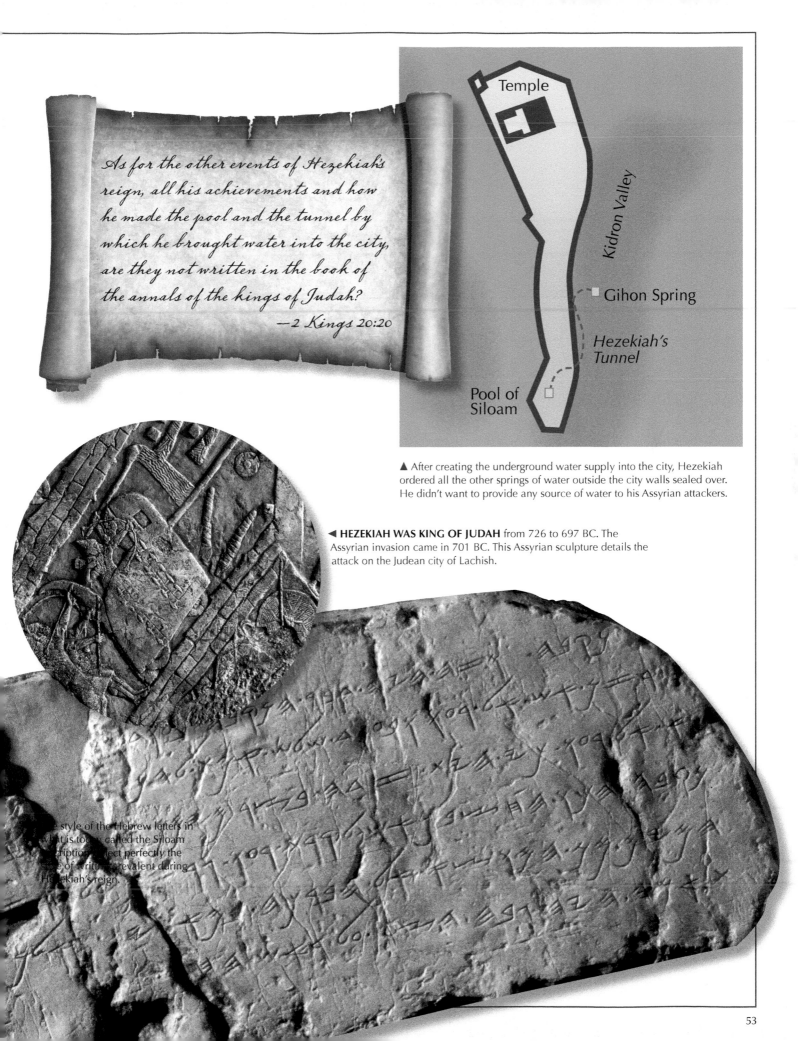

As for the other events of Hezekiah's reign, all his achievements and how he made the pool and the tunnel by which he brought water into the city, are they not written in the book of the annals of the kings of Judah?

—2 Kings 20:20

Temple

Kidron Valley

Gihon Spring

Hezekiah's Tunnel

Pool of Siloam

▲ After creating the underground water supply into the city, Hezekiah ordered all the other springs of water outside the city walls sealed over. He didn't want to provide any source of water to his Assyrian attackers.

◄ **HEZEKIAH WAS KING OF JUDAH** from 726 to 697 BC. The Assyrian invasion came in 701 BC. This Assyrian sculpture details the attack on the Judean city of Lachish.

style of the Hebrew letters in what is today called the Siloam Inscription reflect perfectly the styles of writing prevalent during Hezekiah's reign.

SENNACHERIB'S PRISM

After conquering the smaller cities of Judah, the Assyrian king Sennacherib set his sights on Jerusalem. King Hezekiah's defense strategy had two parts: dig a water tunnel into the city (see *Hezekiah's Tunnel*) and strengthen the outer defenses. Hezekiah ordered a new wall built on the city's west side (2 Chronicles 32:5)—a "Broad Wall" twenty-three feet thick.

Hezekiah also turned to God in repentance and faith. God had spared Jerusalem before, and Hezekiah believed he would do it again. God promised Hezekiah that Sennacherib would return to his own land without capturing Jerusalem. That night an angel of the Lord swept through the Assyrian camp and 185,000 men died. Sennacherib reigned for twenty more years in Nineveh, but he never set foot in Judah again!

Several copies of Sennacherib's annals survive, recorded on six-sided clay prisms and written in Assyrian cuneiform script. Sennacherib put his own political "spin" on what happened in Judah, claiming that he "shut up Hezekiah in Jerusalem, his royal city, like a bird in a cage." But that's the best he can say. He besieged Jerusalem and nothing more! No lists of captured enemies, no descriptions of looting the city, just a silent acknowledgement that he came home empty-handed.

► **SPOILS OF WAR** being taken back to Nineveh after Sennacherib's conquests.

◄ **THIS COPY OF SENNACHERIB'S ANNALS** is called Taylor's Prism because it was discovered in Nineveh in 1830 by British Colonel R. Taylor. It is housed in the British Museum. Another copy is displayed at the Oriental Institute of the University of Chicago and is known as the Oriental Institute Prism.

▼ The walls of the fortress of Lachish, which was destroyed by Sennacherib in 701 B.C.

▼ **KING HEZEKIAH'S NAME** as it appears in the Akkadian language, the language of the Assyrians.

Kha	-	za	-	ki	-	a	-	u		la	-	u	-	da	-	ai
Hezekiah										*of Judah*						

◄ **SENNACHERIB** on his royal throne. He ruled Assyria from 705-681 BC but was eventually assassinated by his own sons.

"By the way that [Sennacherib] came he will return; he will not enter this city, declares the LORD. I will defend this city and save it, for my sake and for the sake of David my servant."

—2 Kings 19:33–34

BROAD WALL

The Broad Wall of Hezekiah was uncovered by Israeli archaeologist, Nahman Avigad, in the early 1970s. The wall was built in such desperation that the people of Jerusalem tore down sections of their own homes and used the stones to fortify the city.

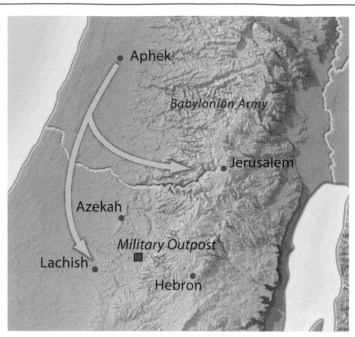

LACHISH LETTERS

The diggers at the biblical city of Lachish uncovered more than the astonishing evidence of the Assyrian attack in 701 BC (see *"War with Assyria"* on page 50). Their most exciting find related to another battle and another invader! More than 100 years after the Assyrian invasion, the Babylonian armies swept through Judah, destroyed the Jewish Temple, and carried off the surviving Jews into exile. The conquest of Jerusalem came at the end of months of grim fighting against the fortified cities of Judah. In the city of Lachish, twenty-one pieces of pottery with writing on them surfaced from the time of the Babylonian attack. These were letters—more like memos—from a subordinate officer who was stationed at an outpost to his commander inside the city of Lachish. Placed alongside the accounts of the conquest in Kings and in the writings of the prophet Jeremiah, the letters convey a powerful sense of the fear and despair that gripped God's people during those devastating days.

▶ **THIS BABYLONIAN TEXT** describes the second of three Babylonian conquests of Judah and Jerusalem. The conquering army was fairly merciful the first time and, even after the second conquest, they left Jerusalem intact. When the Babylonians were forced to come back the third time, however, they destroyed the land and carried the survivors into captivity in Babylon.

JEREMIAH'S ACCURACY IS CONFIRMED – AGAIN!

In the summer of 2007, Dr. Michael Jursa, a visiting professor from the University of Vienna, made a startling discovery in the British Museum's vast collection of clay tablets. He was searching for the names of Babylonian officials when he came upon a name that sounded familiar—Nebo-Sarsekim, the chief eunuch in the court of King Nebuchadnezzar. The same name and title are recorded by Jeremiah for a Babylonian official who was in Jerusalem in 587 BC when Nebuchadnezzar laid siege to the city (Jeremiah 39:3). Nebo-Sarsekim appears only once in the biblical text but, if Jeremiah got it right with the minor details, we can trust him with the bigger facts as well!

▲ **THE TINY TABLET** (a little over two inches wide) is a reciept acknowledging Neb-Sarsekim's extravagant gift of gold to the temple of Esangila in Babylon. It is dated in the tenth year of Nebuchadnezzar (595 BC), eight years before the siege of Jerusalem in 587 BC.

▲ **THE LETTERS** were written by Hoshaiah, the officer in charge of the outpost, to Yaosh, the commander at Lachish. The soldier wrote on pieces of broken pottery—a cheap, common writing surface—with black, iron-carbon ink. Scholars refer to pottery with writing on it as ostraca (singular, ostracon).

◄ **THE KING OF JUDAH** was brought before the Babylonian king, Nebuchadnezzar, and was forced to watch the slaying of his sons. The victors then "put out [Zedekiah's] eyes, bound him with bronze shackles and took him to Babylon" (2 Kings 25:7). It was only after the defeat of Babylon by the Persian armies that the Jews were allowed to return to their homeland.

Jeremiah 34:7

"... Lachish and Azekah; for these were the only fortified cities of Judah that remained."

Letter from a military outpost soldier to the commanding officer in Lachish:

"We are watching for the signals of Lachish ... for we cannot see Azekah."

◄ Daniel's three friends, Shadrach, Meshach, and Abednego, were protected by the "fourth man" in the fiery furnace (Daniel 3). Scholars estimate that 75–100 young men were taken to Babylon in 605 BC, but only four remained true to the Lord God.

MISTAKEN ABOUT DANIEL

Daniel was taken to Babylon as a young teenager, and he lived there more than seventy years under some of Babylon's greatest kings. His book is famous for its stories of heroes who stood true to God. One story tells about a hand appearing in the king's banquet hall and writing a message from God on the wall—a message only Daniel could interpret. In Daniel chapter 5 the Babylonian king who saw "the handwriting on the wall" is called Belshazzar. Here's the problem—the name Belshazzar never appears in the official list of Babylonian kings. In 1850 a German commentator on the book of Daniel declared a little too confidently that Belshazzar was simply a figment of the author's imagination.

Just four years later, however, a British explorer discovered several small clay cylinders in the brickwork of a Babylonian temple. When the writing on the cylinders was translated, a long prayer emerged, a prayer written by Nabonidus, the last recorded king of Babylon, asking for wisdom for his oldest son, Belshazzar. Other documents discovered since then show that Nabonidus disliked the responsibility of leadership and entrusted most of the work to Belshazzar. Nabonidus spent his days at Teima, a military outpost in northern Arabia. Far from being a figment of Daniel's imagination, Belshazzar's name and informal title as "king" demonstrate the incredible accuracy of Daniel's book.

◀ **THE PRAYER OF NABONIDUS** was directed to the god, Sin, "god of gods, who lives in the great heavens." The significant lines read: *As for me, Nabonidus, king of Babylon, save me from sin against your great divinity, and give me life until distant days. And as for Belshazzar, my first born son, my one child, let the fear of your great divinity be in his heart, and may he commit no sin; may he enjoy happiness in life.*

◀ **DANIEL 5** actually confirms the relationship between Nabonidus and Belshazzar. Belshazzar offers to make Daniel *third* ranking ruler in the kingdom (after Belshazzar and his father Nabonidus). The same night Belshazzar made the promise to Daniel, Belshazzar's life was taken by the invading Persian army.

LIST OF BABYLONIAN KINGS DURING DANIEL'S LIFE

Nabopolassar (ruled 626–605 BC)

Daniel born around 620 BC

Nebuchadnezzar (605–562 BC)

Weak kings (562–552 BC)

Nabonidus (552–539 BC) Co-regent: Belshazzar

Daniel lived into the Persian Empire era until at least 535 BC—when he was well into his eighties!

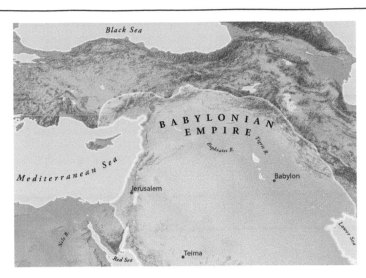

◄ Nabonidus ruled Babylon from 555 BC until the Persian conquest in 539 BC. He seems to have been a very pious man who devoted his time to the worship of the moon god. His ten-year "retreat" at Teima left his weakening empire vulnerable to the Persian threat from the east.

◄ **THE FRAGMENTARY CHRONICLE OF NABONIDUS** helps us understand why the king entrusted rulership to his son, Belshazzar.

◄ **DANIEL WAS TAKEN TO BABYLON** under King Nebuchadnezzar, the great builder of the magnificent capital city. Even the bricks were stamped with the king's name.

◄ Cyrus was killed in battle in 530 BC and his body was transported a thousand miles to this tomb in Pasargadae.

▼ **CYRUS** saw himself as chosen by the god Marduk to remove the tyrant Nabonidus and his son, Belshazzar, from power. Actually the God of heaven used Cyrus to allow the captive people of Israel to return to Jerusalem.

PROPHECY FULFILLED!

▲ **THE FOUR-WINGED CROWNED FIGURE** in this sculpture is believed to be a stylized image of Cyrus. It was found near Cyrus' home city of Pasargadae.

Some discoveries from the ancient world have actually demonstrated the fulfillment of biblical prophecy! Isaiah the prophet predicted that, at the end of Judah's exile in Babylon, a deliverer would set them free and allow them to return to Jerusalem. God even told Isaiah the deliverer's name—Cyrus (Isaiah 44:28; 45:1–2). In time a powerful general arose among the Persians and his armies threw off the oppressive rule of the Babylonians. God's people in exile found themselves under a new power—the Persian empire—and loyal to a new king—Cyrus the Great.

Cyrus allowed the people who had been displaced by the Babylonians to go home. Ezra records Cyrus's decree in Ezra 1—"Whoever there is among you of all his people … let him go up to Jerusalem." Confirmation of Cyrus's release of the captives comes from a Persian document, a nine-inch baked clay cylinder called the Cyrus Cylinder.

"I returned to [these] sacred cities on the other side of the Tigris, the sanctuaries of which have been in ruins for a long time … I also gathered all their [former] inhabitants and returned [to them] their habitations."

What God had promised, God delivered!

ANCIENT EMAIL

The Persian king was the whole Persian government. His decrees were law! In order to get the word out, the Persians established an amazing system of messengers that linked all the major cities of their enormous empire. The book of Esther says, "Dispatches were sent by couriers to all the king's provinces" (Esther 3:13; 10:14).

In 1973 French archaeologists were restoring a temple at Xanthos in southwestern Turkey. At the foot of a wall, they found a stone block over four feet high inscribed in three languages. The first inscription—the original charter of the temple—was written in Greek. On the opposite side of the stone, the same information was inscribed in the local Lycian language. The inscriptions on the other two sides were in Aramaic, the official language of the Persian empire. The inscription demonstrates the difficulty of taking the king's orders to every part of the empire and how the Persians solved that problem by using a team of translators to render the king's decrees into dozens of languages. "Their orders were written in the script of each province and the language of each people" (Esther 8:9).

▼ **JUDAH'S KING, JEHOIACHIN,** was taken to Babylon in 597 BC (2 Kings 24:15), but he was soon released from arrest and found himself supported at government expense. This document fragment from Babylon mentions Jehoiachin by name and lists provision of food for the king and his family.

► **THIS SILVER AMULET** (shown here unrolled) was discovered near Jerusalem and dates from the time of the exile. Apparently the area around Jerusalem was not totally deserted during those years. What made this discovery so exciting was the presence in writing of God's covenant name, Yahweh.

CLIFF-SIDE CARVING

For centuries, travelers on the caravan road going west from Teheran stood amazed at the figures carved in the side of the cliff almost 300 feet above their heads. They thought it must have been drawn by the finger of God. A tall figure of a man raises his hand toward ten men in front of

him while two men stand behind him. A strange bird-like image hovers above them. Beside the portrait the rock was polished smooth—or at least it appeared smooth from 300 feet below. Upon closer examination, the rock was found to be covered with thousands of tiny arrow-head shaped marks chiseled into the stone. Scholars decided that it was an ancient form of writing and called it *cuneiform* (**que**-nee-form; a Latin term meaning "wedge-shaped").

The mountainside writing sparked the interest of people across Europe in the 1830s and 1840s. Finally, scholars concluded that the inscription preserved the same text in three languages—Old Persian, Babylonian, and Elamite. The rock helped break the code of these difficult, long-forgotten languages and opened up the abundant records from Assyria and Babylonia. Those documents in turn threw astonishing new light on the world of the Old Testament. Suddenly kings and battles and empires mentioned in Scripture took on new form and reality—and the Bible's accuracy in describing those events and people was confirmed over and over again.

◀ **A SCULPTURE OF XERXES** (called Ahasuerus in the book of Esther) at the entrance to his throne room in Persepolis.

▲ **THOUSANDS OF DOCUMENTS WRITTEN IN CUNEIFORM** have been recovered from Assyrian, Babylonian, and Persian sites—but only about 10 percent of them have been translated.

▲ **THE ROCK CARVING NEAR THE CITY OF BEHISTUN** is a tribute to Darius the Great who ruled the Persian Empire from 522 until 486 BC. Under his rule, the Jews in exile returned to Jerusalem and rebuilt God's temple. The large figure is Darius, and the two men behind him are his trusted aides. The ten smaller figures in front of Darius (and under his feet) are conquered kings. The winged figure is the god Ahuramazda overseeing it all.

▲ **THE TEXT OF THE INSCRIPTION** also mentions Xerxes, who succeeded Darius on the Persian throne and who made Esther the Jewess his queen.

◄ **THE BRITISH EXPLORER HENRY RAWLINSON** copied the inscription at great personal risk—standing at the top of tall ladders and swinging from rope slings! The difficulty he encountered just reading and copying the inscription gave him great admiration for those who made the carving in the first place.

► **BEHISTUN** is the location of this magnificent carving. Persepolis is the ancient capital of the Persian Empire. The map gives us some sense of the expanse of Persian rule—before cell phones, CNN, or email!

▲ The slaughter in Bethlehem was just one example of Herod's murderous ways. He executed three of his sons, his wife, and his mother-in-law, along with dozens of his political enemies.

HEROD: MURDERER, DREAMER, KING

As the New Testament opens, we come face to face with a mad man. His name was Herod, but he preferred to be called

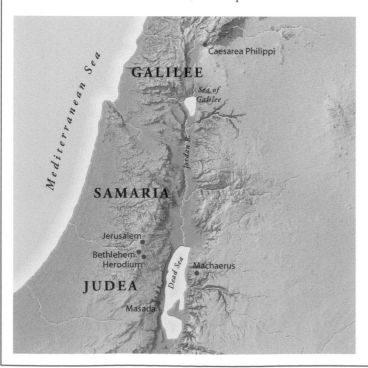

▲ THE AMAZING ROCK FORTRESS OF MASADA became the final stronghold for Jewish zealots during the war against Rome in AD 67–70. The Zealots on Masada held off the Roman legions until AD 73—and then committed suicide to keep from being captured.

Herod the Great! When magi from the east came to Jerusalem in search of the newborn king of the Jews, Herod responded by ordering his troops to kill all the male babies in Bethlehem (Matthew 2:13–18). A few months later, Herod died. What the New Testament doesn't tell you directly is that Herod and his family left a deep mark on the people of Israel and on the land of the Bible itself.

Herod and his sons and grandsons ruled the region of Judea for more than one hundred years (from 37 BC until around AD 100). They crossed paths at various times with Jesus, Peter, James, and Paul. Grandpa Herod accumulated enormous wealth and spent most of it on lavish building projects. You couldn't travel anywhere in Israel without being near one of the magnificent palaces or fortresses he built for his enjoyment and protection.

MORE HERODS

Herod Agrippa I, grandson of Herod the Great, had the apostle James executed and Peter imprisoned (Acts 12:1–4). Agrippa's son and daughter, Herod Agrippa II and Bernice, listened to Paul preach in Acts 25. Young Agrippa's response to Paul's invitation to believe in Jesus was: "Do you think that in such a short time you can persuade me to be a Christian?"

◄ **THE LOWER PART OF ONE TOWER** is all that remains of the Citadel, Herod's luxurious palace in Jerusalem. The palace eventually became the residence of the Roman governor, the Praetorium, where Jesus was condemned. The Praetorium (also called the Fortress of Antonia) was also the place where Paul was taken after his arrest in the temple area (Acts 22:23–24).

▼ A sixteenth-century depiction by Andrea Solaris of Herod Antipas presenting the head of John the Baptist to Salome, his stepdaughter. Salome had asked for John's execution after performing a provocative dance for Herod and his guests at a birthday banquet (Matthew 14:1–12).

▼ **THE APOSTLE PETER** made a remarkable confession of faith in Jesus at Caesarea Philippi (Matthew 16:13–20). Herod's son, Philip, had enlarged the city of Paneas and renamed it in honor of the emperor and himself.

▲ Herod built the Herodium around 24 BC as both a palace and a fortress. On a hill southeast of Bethlehem, workmen constructed an elaborate round fort that could only be reached by climbing 200 steps to the doorway.

A PLACE TO DIE

Machaerus is the exact place where John the Baptist was imprisoned and executed by Herod's son, Herod Antipas (Mark 6). At Jesus' trial, Pontius Pilate tried to push the decision about Jesus over to Herod Antipas because Jesus was from Galilee, the territory Herod ruled. Jesus, however, refused to speak to John the Baptist's executioner (Luke 23:6–12).

TRIP TO THE TEMPLE

The temple is the setting for several key events in the Gospels and the book of Acts:

• Jesus as a boy asks questions of the Jewish teachers (Luke 2:41–50).

• Jesus cleanses the temple of its commercial operations—twice (John 2:12–22; Matthew 21:12–13).

• Jesus' disciples praise the temple's beauty and are stunned by Jesus' prediction of the temple's destruction (Mark 13:1–2).

• Peter and John heal a lame man at one of the temple gates (Acts 3:1–10).

• Paul's presence in the temple starts a riot (Acts 21:26–36).

▲ This modern scale model (above) gives us some idea of how impressive and awe-inspiring the temple was. Visitors to Jerusalem stood speechless at their first sight.

▶ **THIS TINY SUNDIAL** (2 inches by 2 inches) is the only surviving object from the second Jewish temple. It was probably used to calculate the time of the daily offerings.

HEROD'S TEMPLE

Herod's most impressive building project was his expansion and beautification of Israel's worship center in Jerusalem. The temple is the one building referred to most often in the New Testament. The original temple built by King Solomon was destroyed by the armies of Babylon in 586 BC. A "second" temple was built when the Jews returned from captivity in Babylon, but it was small and unimpressive. Herod set out to restore the glory and majesty of the original temple, but it was no quick makeover. He started the project in 20 BC, and it was still going on during Jesus' ministry, thirty years after Herod's death. The restoration was not fully completed until AD 63, just seven years before the Romans destroyed the entire temple area. Not much survived the crushing destruction of the temple but what we have found are stunning reminders of the overwhelming beauty of that magnificent worship center.

► ON THE WESTERN WALL OF THE TEMPLE COMPLEX, a magnificent arch supported a stairway from the street level to the courtyard of the temple far above. During an expedition in 1838, an American historian, Edward Robinson, discovered some stones projecting from the wall and realized that they were all that remained of the Great Arch.

► The expanded platform where the temple stood is now occupied by the Dome of the Rock and the al-Aqsa mosque—sites revered by Muslims.

▲ Herod looking at plans for expanding the temple.

LOST TREASURES OF THE TEMPLE

Legends have circulated for two thousand years about what happened to the treasures of the Second Temple. Most scholars believe that the Roman armies took everything of value and burned the rest to the ground. In 1953 an unusual scroll was discovered in one of the caves where the Dead Sea Scrolls were found. All the other scrolls were made of parchment (leather) and a few were papyrus (similar to paper) but this scroll was made of copper. It took years to unroll the deteriorated copper but finally experts sawed the scroll into sections with a jeweler's saw and were able to read the engraving. The scroll revealed a detailed list of sixty-four secret locations where priests had carefully hidden the gold and silver from the Temple. The treasures included a number of sacred vessels, manuscripts, and the breastplate of the high priest. A number of Dead Sea Scroll archaeologists have concluded that the treasure is not real, only imagined. None of the hiding places has ever been located with certainty, and no gold or silver hoards have ever been found—but who knows what the next digger's spade might uncover!

◄ THE ONLY PART OF THE SECOND TEMPLE that remains intact today is a section of the foundation of the western wall. Jews call it the Wailing Wall and view it as a sacred place of prayer.

▼ THE ARCH OF TITUS in Rome commemorates the Roman victory in the Jewish wars. One panel shows the menorah (lamp stand) from the temple being paraded before the Roman crowds.

JEWS ONLY

Within the walls of Herod's temple in Jerusalem, a huge open area called the Court of Gentiles admitted anyone who want-ed to see the grandeur of Israel's worship center. The actual sacred temple, however, was separated off by other walls and courts. Between the Court of Gentiles and the Court of Women, a four-and-a-half foot stone barrier was erected, and notices in Greek and Latin were placed at each entrance. The temple no longer exists, but some of the original warning signs have been found.

Only Jews were to cross into the inner courts. Non-Jews (Gentiles) who dared to set foot inside were likely to be stoned by zealous guardians of Jewish tradition. The apostle Paul was accused of exactly that crime in the book of Acts. Jews who were opposed to Paul's message of salvation to Gentiles claimed that he brought a non-Jew, a man named Trophimus, into the temple area and, as a result, had desecrated the temple (Acts 21:28–29).

◄ **ONE COMPLETE AND TWO FRAGMENTARY COPIES** of the warning signs have been discovered. All the ones that have been found are written in Greek. The text reads: "No foreigner [Gentile] is to enter within the balustrade [wall] and embankment around the sanctuary. Whoever is caught will have himself to blame for his death which follows."

◄ This fhis frragagmentment of a warning sign shows that originally the letters were painted red—the ancient world's equivalent to a fl ashing red light!

► **A SIGN FROM THE SECOND TEMPLE** that directed people "to the trumpeting place"—the spot where the priests sounded the shofar, calling Israel to worship.

▲ Jesus often used the temple as a place to teach and heal even though it usually ended in a debate with the religious leaders.

▲ **THE EARLY CHRISTIANS** met in an area of the Court of Gentiles called "Solomon's Colonnade"—a covered area where groups could gather for worship or instruction (Acts 5:12).

GIVING TO GOD

This bone box was discovered in 1902 on the Mount of Olives. The inscription reads: "Bones of the sons of Nicanor the Alexandrian who made the doors." Nicanor donated a set of magnifi cent doors for the eastern entrance to the temple. Covered in bronze rather than gold, the craftsmanship was so superb that they were considered more valuable than any of the other gates. The doors were also incredibly heavy and required twenty strong men to open and close them each day. The doors are gone, but Nicanor's name—and his spirit of gener-osity—lives on.

▲ What has come to be called the "Jesus boat" is housed at a museum near the place it was discovered.

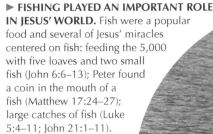

▶ **FISHING PLAYED AN IMPORTANT ROLE IN JESUS' WORLD.** Fish were a popular food and several of Jesus' miracles centered on fish: feeding the 5,000 with five loaves and two small fish (John 6:6–13); Peter found a coin in the mouth of a fish (Matthew 17:24–27); large catches of fish (Luke 5:4–11; John 21:1–11).

◀ **THE ORIGINAL VESSEL** was 26 ½ feet long, 7 ½ feet wide and 4 ½ feet high—a typical round-bottom, one-masted fishing boat of Jesus' day.

THE JESUS BOAT

A two-year drought in Israel in 1986 lowered the water level in the Sea of Galilee. Two brothers walking the shoreline saw an interesting oval outline in the mud—a fishing boat had been preserved under water for 2,000 years!

Carbon–14 dating of the wood and the objects found near the boat confirm that the vessel was built somewhere between 100 BC and AD 70. It was powered by both a sail and oars and was used primarily for commercial fishing. The boat normally carried five or six crew members but was capable of carrying as many as fifteen—just the right size for the trips Jesus and his twelve disciples made across the Sea of Galilee.

Did Jesus actually sail—or sleep (Mark 4:37)—in this boat? The scholar who directed the preservation said the odds are 1 in 1,000 that Jesus ever set foot in this particular vessel, but it certainly allows us to see what it was like to sail on the Sea of Galilee when Jesus and his followers were there.

▲ **AT LEAST FOUR OF JESUS' CLOSEST FOLLOWERS** were experienced fishermen—Peter, Andrew, James, and John. Medieval fresco by Duccio di Buoninsegna.

▲ This mosaic of a first-century fishing boat is on display in Capernaum.

◄ **THE WATERLOGGED FIBERS IN THE WOOD** were strengthened by infusing a synthetic wax-like substance. It took preservationists twelve years to stabilize the fragile structure. The boat was either salvaged for parts after its useful life was over, or it was sunk in the Roman-Jewish war of AD 67–70. Josephus, a Jewish historian, says that the shore of the Sea of Galilee was littered with wrecks.

◀ Modern Jews still read from meticulously copied scrolls of the Hebrew Bible.

THE BIBLE JESUS READ

When the documents now called the Dead Sea Scrolls were found, a beautiful scroll of the book of Isaiah was one of the treasures that stunned the world. Here was a manuscript one thousand years older than our oldest Hebrew Bible! It was a scroll written and read in the time of Jesus and the early apostles.

When Jesus visited the synagogue in his hometown of Nazareth, he asked to read from the scroll of Isaiah—a hand-printed scroll on smooth leather very much like the one discovered near the Dead Sea. Jesus unrolled the scroll to the place where he wanted to read and publicly proclaimed that he was the fulfillment of what Isaiah had written 700 years earlier (Luke 4:16–19). The Dead Sea Scrolls have not only shed amazing light on Jewish life in Jesus' day; they have also given us a glimpse of the Bible Jesus read and loved and memorized.

▶ This is the only surviving writing stylus from the area of Qumran where the Dead Sea Scrolls originated. It is made from a palm leaf that has a natural groove for the ink.

◄ **THE SCRIPTORIUM** is most likely the room at Qumran where devout Jewish scribes copied biblical texts and the important documents of their community.

▼ **A COLUMN OF THE ISAIAH SCROLL** Pieces of leather were sewn together to make a scroll long enough to contain the entire text of the book of Isaiah.

▼ The dry, hot desert climate around the Dead Sea helped to preserve the documents for almost two thousand years.

▲ **AFTER JESUS CLAIMED TO BE THE FULFILLMENT OF ISAIAH'S PROPHECY,** the people of Nazareth were so offended that they brought him out to this hill to push him from the cliff—but Jesus escaped (Luke 4:28–30).

PONTIUS PILATE

The man who condemned Jesus to death was a Roman career officer who ruled Judea for ten years (AD 26–36). His official residence was in the city of Caesarea Maritima on the Mediterranean coast. In 1961, as Italian scholars excavated Caesarea's ancient Roman theater, they discovered a stone plaque bearing Pilate's name. The monument had been carved to commemorate Pilate's construction of the Tiberium, a temple for the worship of Tiberius Caesar, the reigning Roman emperor.

The Pilate Inscription, as it came to be called, is the first artifact that mentions Pilate by name. Pilate's habit of insulting the religious sensitivity of the Jews eventually led to his recall to Rome. Unfortunately for Pilate, his friend, Emperor Tiberius, died before he arrived. The new emperor, Caligula, exiled Pilate to Gaul (modern France) where tradition says that Pilate committed suicide.

▼ Judea was a third class imperial province—a small, relatively poor, highly volatile district on the eastern frontier of the Roman Empire. Not a very promising place for a career-minded politician!

▲ **THE TRADITIONAL LOCATION** where Pilate tried to elicit sympathy for Jesus from the crowd saying, "Behold the man!" (or "Ecce homo" in Latin).

◄ **THE TWO-FOOT BY THREE-FOOT SLAB** had been reused in a fourth century remodeling project—but it is an authentic first century inscription. Even though some of the inscription is broken away, Pilate's name and title are clearly seen. The translation of the Latin text is: "[This] house for Tiberius / [Pon]tius Pilate / [Pre]fect of Judea [built]."

[...............]S TIBERIUM
[PON]TIUS PILATUS
[PRAEF]ECTUS JUDA[EA]E
[FOR] TIBERIUS
[BY PON]TIUS PILATE
[PRAEF]ECT OF JUDEA

▲ A classic portrait by Antonio
Ciseri of Pilate presenting Jesus to
the crowd.

▼ **CAESAREA MARITIMA WAS THE CAPITAL** city of the Roman
province of Judea. It was far more influenced by Roman culture
than the city of Jerusalem which was dominated by orthodox
Jews. Pilate journeyed to Jerusalem only at times of high tension in
the city—like during the festival of Passover.

▼ **PILATE ISSUED THREE
BRONZE COINS** during his rule.
He was the only Roman ruler to use
pagan symbols on money issued for
commercial use among strictly Jewish people. The curved staff (or *lituus*)
pictured on this coin was carried by pagan Roman priests.

▼ **THE BURIAL OF YOHANAN IN A FAMILY TOMB** demonstrates that crucified victims could receive a proper burial—as Jesus was buried in the tomb of Joseph of Arimathea. Since crucified victims had been condemned as criminals, most of their bodies were simply thrown down the side of the execution hill to be eaten by scavenging animals.

CRUCIFIXION

The ancient Assyrians are the ones who first came up with crucifixion as a way to torture their enemies, but the Romans perfected it as a method of slow, brutal execution. At times hundreds, even thousands, of Rome's enemies were crucified at once, but no direct evidence of a crucified victim was ever found in the area of Judea until 1968. An ossuary (or bone box) was found north of Jerusalem that contained the remains of Yohanan ben Ha'galgol. This thirty-year-old man's right anklebone was still pierced with a seven-inch nail. When the man was crucified, the nail apparently hit a knot in the olive wood cross and became so imbedded that the man's body could not be removed without taking the nail and some of the wood with it. The bone makes the horror and suffering of Jesus' crucifixion even more real.

► **THIS FIRST CENTURY PAVING STONE** was inscribed with a Roman game, "The Game of Kings," and may have come from the Roman fortress in Jerusalem where Jesus was condemned. It may have been a crude form of this game that the Roman soldiers played as they gambled for Jesus' tunic (John 19:23–24).

VIA DOLOROSA

The route through Jerusalem from Pilate's fortress to the place of crucifixion is a popular tourist site. The pathway is called the Via Dolorosa, the way of sorrows.

◄ **RATHER THAN NAILING** through the top of the victim's feet as is usually depicted, it is likely that the legs were bent, pushed up, and nailed together through the ankles. Pictured here is the ankle bone of Yohanan ben Ha'galgol with the Roman nail still in place.

▲ **GOLGOTHA** is one proposed location of the crucifixion of Jesus near Jerusalem.

▼ **JESUS' CRUCIFIXION** was preceded by a whipping with a Roman scourge. Pieces of bone or metal imbedded in the leather thongs ripped the victim's flesh.

EVERYDAY TREASURES

Gold jewelry and ancient inscriptions are wonderful finds for an archaeologist, but common, ordinary treasures can tell us just as much about the world of the Bible. Stone jars, for instance, play a key role in Jesus' first miracle at a wedding in Cana. When the host family ran out of wine (a serious insult to their guests), Jesus instructed the servants to fill six stone jars with water (John 2:6). When the servants drew the water back out, it had been miraculously changed into wine. Excavators have found several such jars in the ruins of first century Jewish homes. They were designed to hold the large quantities of water needed for ritual washing and for cooking.

▼ Alabaster Jars used to store perfumes and oils.

"His two months are (olive) harvest,
His two months are planting (grain),
His two months are late planting,
His month is hoeing up flax,
His month is harvest of barley,
His month is harvest and feasting,
His two months are vine tending,
His month is summer fruit."

(Translation by William F. Albright)

▼ **A LIMESTONE TABLET** found in the Israelite city of Gezer was probably a school child's writing exercise. The text is a folk song describing the months of the year in an agricultural society.

LOVE IN A BOTTLE

Expensive perfumes and aromatic oils were stored in stone bottles to protect the contents from evaporation. Mary of Bethany, who anointed Jesus, broke open an alabaster jar of oil valued at more than a year's salary (Mark 14:3–5; John 12:1–6). The long neck of the container could be broken, releasing all the perfume at once and filling the house with its fragrance.

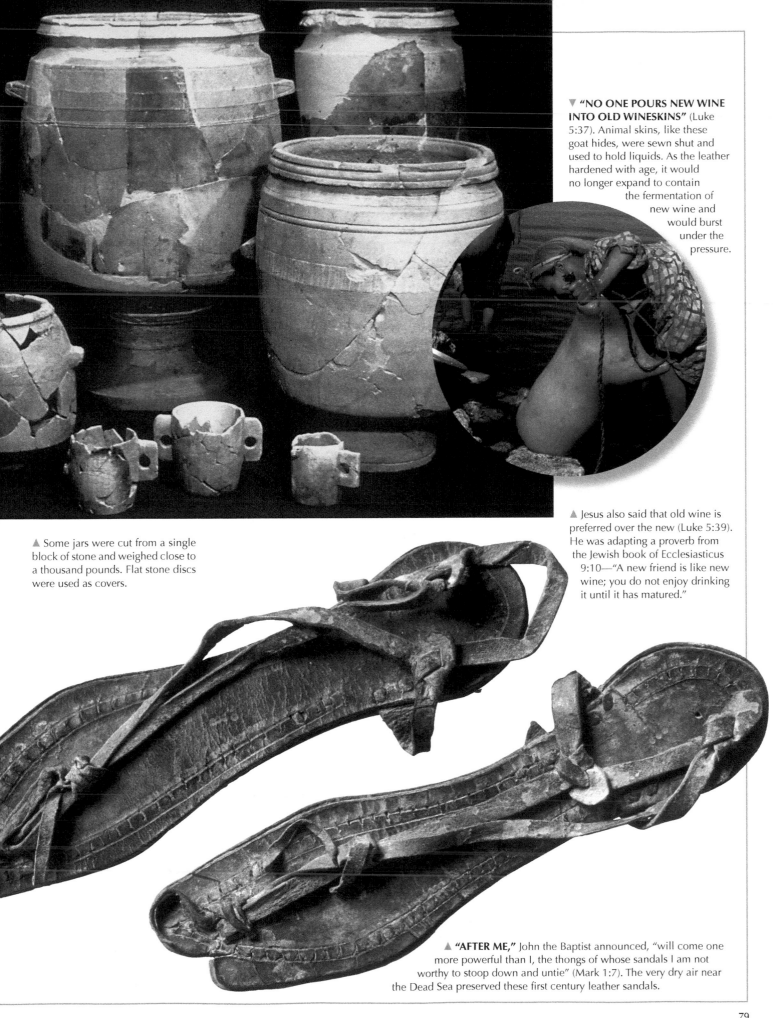

"NO ONE POURS NEW WINE INTO OLD WINESKINS" (Luke 5:37). Animal skins, like these goat hides, were sewn shut and used to hold liquids. As the leather hardened with age, it would no longer expand to contain the fermentation of new wine and would burst under the pressure.

▲ Some jars were cut from a single block of stone and weighed close to a thousand pounds. Flat stone discs were used as covers.

▲ Jesus also said that old wine is preferred over the new (Luke 5:39). He was adapting a proverb from the Jewish book of Ecclesiasticus 9:10—"A new friend is like new wine; you do not enjoy drinking it until it has matured."

▲ **"AFTER ME,"** John the Baptist announced, "will come one more powerful than I, the thongs of whose sandals I am not worthy to stoop down and untie" (Mark 1:7). The very dry air near the Dead Sea preserved these first century leather sandals.

FAMOUS FACES

Long before television and *USA Today*, politicians had a desire to be in the public eye. The easiest way to get your image in front of people was to produce coins imprinted with your name and your "picture." Americans would recognize Thomas Jefferson and Andrew Jackson because we handle their images every day. The British and Canadians honor the Queen by printing her likeness on their money. Ancient rulers did the same thing—and their coins put faces on some well-known biblical names.

▶ **TIBERIUS**—Roman emperor during Jesus' adulthood and ministry (AD 14–37). This coin is similar to the one that Jesus held up when he said, "Give to Caesar what is Caesar's, and to God what is God's" (Matthew 22:17–21).

▶ **BECAUSE THE JEWS** were less likely to tolerate a coin with a human or animal image on it, Herod the Great, who ruled Judea from 37 to 4 BC, issued this coin decorated with a ceremonial bowl and inscribed "to King Herod" in Greek.

Citizens in the Roman Empire were required to use the silver denarius which bore the emperor's image to pay their taxes. The Jewish people had to use the coin whether they liked it or not.

▼ **HEROD AGRIPPA I,** ruler of Judea from AD 37–44 and grandson of Herod the Great, was the Judean ruler who had the apostle James killed and the apostle Peter imprisoned (Acts 12:1–23; 23:35).

▼ **ARETAS IV,** king of the Nabateans (9 BC—AD 40), whose governor in Damascus attempted to arrest Paul (2 Corinthians 11:32).

THE WIDOW'S MITE

The most famous coins in the Bible were worth almost nothing! As Jesus sat in the temple treasury area, a poor woman cast two "mites" into the offering (Mark 12:41–44). These tiny copper coins represented all that the woman had. Rather than ridiculing her gift, Jesus praised her as an example of a sacrificial giver—exactly the kind of giver God rejoices to see! The woman would not have starved by giving the last of her money because the Jewish people made provisions for the care of widows through their synagogues —but she willingly gave all she had to live on as an act of sacrifice and faith in God.

▼ **CLAUDIUS**—Roman emperor who ordered Jews, including Aquila and Priscilla, to leave Rome (AD 41–54; Acts 11:28; 17:7; 18:2).

▼ **CAESAR AUGUSTUS** (ruled 27 BC– AD 14) —The Roman emperor when Jesus was born (Luke 2:1). Augustus had ordered the tax census that brought Joseph and Mary from Galilee to Bethlehem at just the right time for Jesus to be born in David's city.

BONE BOXES

▲ The James ossuary was not discovered in its original site. It came from an Israeli antiquities dealer who did not have the best reputation for authenticity.

In 2002 world media announced "the most significant biblical discovery ever made." It was a bone box, an ossuary, carefully inscribed with these words: "James, the son of Joseph, the brother of Jesus." This was the burial box of the half-brother (or step-brother) of Jesus. James was a leader in the early church and the writer of our New Testament letter of James. The discovery of his burial box was exciting in itself. What stunned the world, however, was the reference to Jesus. This was the oldest historical reference to Jesus ever found, closer to Jesus' actual life than even the earliest copies of the New Testament Gospels.

Since the first days of the ossuary's appearance, some scholars have raised serious questions about the authenticity of the inscription. Israeli authorities at first accepted it as the real thing, but later they labeled it a counterfeit. Other scholars who have studied the inscription closely insist that it is authentic—a clear reference to three key New Testament characters.

◀ There is little doubt that the ossuary is a genuine first-century artifact. What scholars question is the inscription. It reads in neatly carved Aramaic: Ya'akov, son of Yosef, brother of Yeshua.

The problem is that the engraving seems to have been done by two different writers. "James, the son of Joseph" is standard first-century Aramaic; "the brother of Jesus" appears to be a clumsier attempt to add words that make the inscription so significant.

Yeshua	brother of	Yosef	son of	Ya'akov

Text reads from right to left

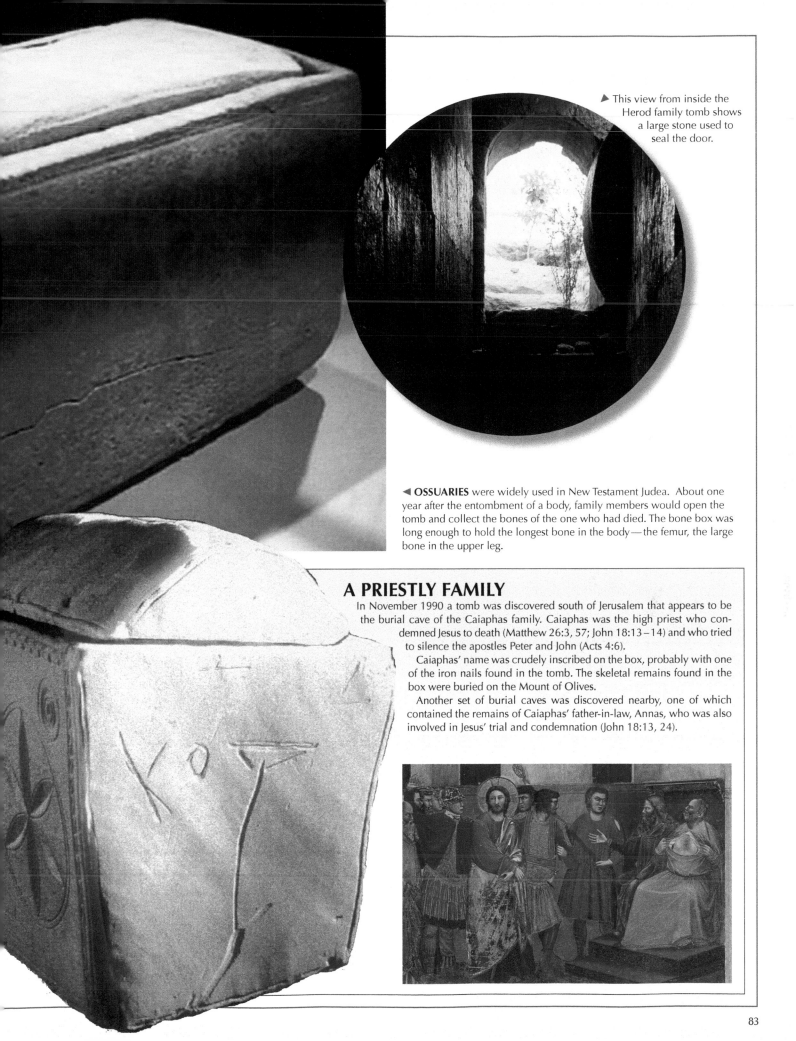

▶ This view from inside the Herod family tomb shows a large stone used to seal the door.

◀ **OSSUARIES** were widely used in New Testament Judea. About one year after the entombment of a body, family members would open the tomb and collect the bones of the one who had died. The bone box was long enough to hold the longest bone in the body—the femur, the large bone in the upper leg.

A PRIESTLY FAMILY

In November 1990 a tomb was discovered south of Jerusalem that appears to be the burial cave of the Caiaphas family. Caiaphas was the high priest who condemned Jesus to death (Matthew 26:3, 57; John 18:13–14) and who tried to silence the apostles Peter and John (Acts 4:6).

Caiaphas' name was crudely inscribed on the box, probably with one of the iron nails found in the tomb. The skeletal remains found in the box were buried on the Mount of Olives.

Another set of burial caves was discovered nearby, one of which contained the remains of Caiaphas' father-in-law, Annas, who was also involved in Jesus' trial and condemnation (John 18:13, 24).

► **CONDEMNED TO DEATH BY NERO,** Peter, tradition says, asked to be crucified upside down. He did not consider himself worthy to be crucified in the same manner as Jesus. Peter's crucifixion was predicted in Jesus' words to him in John 21:18—"when you are old you will stretch out your hands, and someone else will . . . lead you where you do not want to go."

▼ **THE WALLS OF THE FIRST CENTURY ROOM** were marked with Christian graffiti—prayers and words of praise to God, written by believers in the early centuries of the church.

▲ **AFTER PETER'S EXECUTION IN ROME,** his body was buried on Vatican Hill next to Nero's "circus"—an arena for races and games. Early Christians venerated the spot and progressively larger churches were built over the area. In 1939 Vatican authorities secretly authorized excavations below Saint Peter's basilica and discovered human bones dating from the first century. Catholic authorities believe that they are the remains of Peter.

PETER'S HOUSE

What would it be like to stand in the exact place where Jesus stood—or to be in the very room where Jesus had performed a powerful miracle of healing? Archaeologists have found places just like that in the town of Capernaum on the shore of the Sea of Galilee. The synagogue was a place Jesus visited and preached in several times over the course of his public ministry (John 6:59). The first century worship building where Jesus spoke was eventually replaced, but the foundation of the original building is still there.

Even more startling was the discovery of the house where Simon Peter lived. Less than a hundred feet from the synagogue, an octagonal church marked a spot revered by Christians for hundreds of years. Beneath the floor of the church, discoverers found the walls of a room dating back to the time of Jesus, possibly the same room where Jesus had healed Peter's mother-in-law of a fever (Matthew 8:14–15).

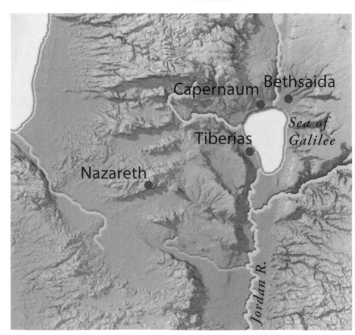

Capernaum   Bethsaida

Tiberias   *Sea of Galilee*

Nazareth

Jordan R.

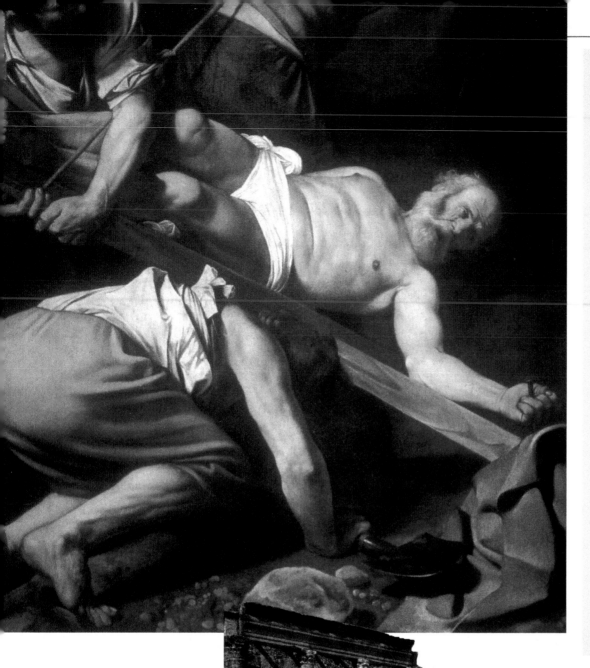

MIRACLES OF JESUS AT CAPERNAUM

- Dead daughter of Jairus raised (Mark 5:22; Luke 8:41)

- Evil spirit driven from a man in the synagogue (Mark 1:21–28)

- Paralyzed man let down through the roof and healed (Mark 2:1–2)

- Jesus causes four disciples to catch a large haul of fish (Luke 5:1–11)

- Jesus supplied tax money to Peter through a fish (Matthew 17:24–27)

- Centurion's servant is healed (Matthew 8:5–13)

- Nobleman's son is healed (John 4:46–54)

- Healing of many others (Mark 1:29–34)

A STRONG FOUNDATION

Underneath the white limestone walls of a later synagogue, archaeologists have uncovered the original foundation made of a black basalt stone. This was likely the synagogue given to the town by a Roman centurion whose servant Jesus healed (Luke 7:4–5).

SIGHTSEEING IN CORINTH

Corinth was the sin city of the ancient world! The city was also situated at one of the crossroads of the Roman empire.

Commerce by land traveled north and south through the narrow strip of land connecting Achaia and Macedonia. Shipping ports on the east and on the west brought goods and travelers from every region of the world. Paul saw Corinth as a great place for a church!

A man named Erastus came to believe in Jesus during Paul's year and a half stay in Corinth (Acts 18:11). One of the paving stones from the city's theater district contains part of a Latin inscription that reads: "Erastus in return for his aedileship [an important city office] laid (the pavement) at his own expense." Paul mentions Erastus in his letter to the Roman Christians, a letter written from Corinth: "Erastus, who is the city's director of public works,... sends you greetings" (Romans 16:23). Erastus appears two more times in the New Testament—as Paul's companion in Ephesus (Acts 19:22) and as a friend left behind in Corinth when Paul was taken to Rome (2 Timothy 4:20).

◄ MOST CORINTHIANS
WERE PAGANS—worshippers
of the gods of Greek or Roman
mythology. The Temple of Apollo,
located near the city center, was
built 600 years before Paul's
arrival.

► **PAUL FOUND A THRIVING JEWISH SYNAGOGUE IN CORINTH** This inscription may have appeared above the door or at a nearby intersection—"Synagogue of the Hebrews."

RUNNING TO WIN!

Paul was an avid sports fan! During his stay in Corinth he had the chance to watch athletes prepare for the Isthmian Games—a competition second only to the Olympics in ancient Greece. Paul used several athletic images to picture the Christian life, including boxing, wrestling, and most often, running. Christians are called to endure the rigors of training and self-denial so we can run the race of following Christ with energy and purpose. The end of the race brings a magnificent reward. "[Athletes] do it to get a crown that will not last; but we do it to get a crown that will last forever" (1 Corinthians 9:25). In the games at Corinth the prize was a crown of pine branches; for the Christian, the reward is the approval of the King!

► This sign directed people to a meat market attached to a pagan temple. Paul dealt extensively in First Corinthians with the issue of eating meat that had been offered to idols.

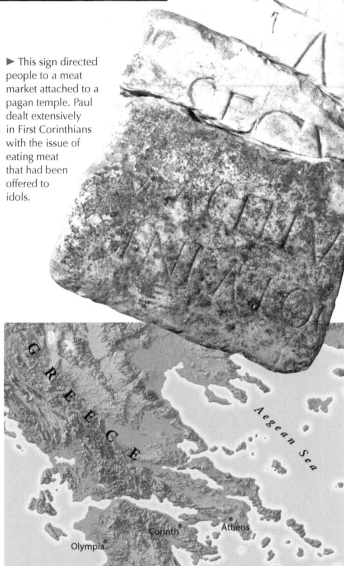

▲ Map of the Greek peninsula showing Corinth's favorable location for trade by land and by sea.

◄ **THE LECHAION ROAD** was a wide (20–25 feet) paved highway that connected the western harbor on the Corinthian Gulf with the marketplace—a road Paul and the early Christians at Corinth used frequently.

TOURING EPHESUS

▲ The apostle John lived in Ephesus for many years and was honored as the last living apostle of Jesus.

First century Ephesus was a magnificent city. The apostle Paul visited the city several times on his journeys and at one point lived in Ephesus for three years (Acts 20:31). Paul and his companions would have found a bustling metro area of two hundred thousand people (huge by ancient standards) filled with the sounds of commerce and the sights of lavish prosperity. The most impressive sight was the temple of Artemis. It was the first religious structure built entirely of marble and the largest building in the entire Greek world. Paul's call to believe in the one true God prompted a riot among the worshippers of Artemis. For two hours they shouted the greatness of their fertility goddess (Acts 19:34). Remains of the actual agora or marketplace where Paul preached and the open-air theater where the Artemis demonstration took place can still be seen in Ephesus.

Among Paul's friends in the city were powerful politicians called *asiarchs* (Acts 19:31). Further discovery has confirmed the names of at least 106 men and women who functioned as asiarchs in Ephesus. These wealthy and influential leaders directed the affairs of the city and funded public games for the entertainment of the people. Luke's historical accuracy is confirmed again!

◄ The Roman-style theater where 24,000 shouting Ephesians protested Paul's preaching about Jesus.

► **ARTEMIS** is the mother goddess and so she is usually depicted with multiple breasts as a sign of her role as the nurturing spirit of nature.

▶ The commercial marketplace or agora, located in the heart of Ephesus, was renovated by both Augustus and Nero as a gift to the citizens of the city.

▶ **ONLY THE FOUNDATION** and one column of the Temple of Artemis remain. In 1863 the British Museum sent John Wood to search for the temple—a search that took him six years to complete! The massive temple was one of the seven wonders of the ancient world.

THE APOSTLE JOHN

Early church tradition says that the apostle John spent his last years in Ephesus and that he wrote his Gospel and his letters from that city. John was the only apostle to die of old age rather than to be martyred for the faith. By the second century, a small church marked John's tomb. The remains of that church are pictured above.

TAFRI BVS ... DIMISSVS E IN SPORTA

LOWERED IN A BASKET

Paul's troubles began within days of his conversion! When his former allies in Damascus heard that Paul had converted and now believed in Jesus as the Messiah, they plotted to kill him. The gates of Damascus were watched day and night. The Christians secretly lowered Paul over the city wall (left) in a basket (Acts 9:23–25). This section of the old city wall is believed to be the exact location where Paul made his escape.

▲ Artwork of Paul being lowered in a basket over the Damascus wall.

▶ PAUL IN 2 CORINTHIANS 11:25 says that he was beaten three times with rods. Roman officials carried bundles of rods (called fasces) as a sign of their authority—and the rods were used to flog those who crossed that authority!

PAUL IN TROUBLE

Paul seemed to get in trouble wherever he went. He didn't check out the motels in a new city until he had checked out the jail because he would probably end up there! None of us wants to spend the night in a Roman jail, but what would it be like to stand in the places where Paul stood?

When a riot started in Corinth, for example, Paul was dragged before the Roman proconsul of the province, a man named Gallio (Acts 18:12–17). The man judged Paul's case while seated on a bema, a large stone platform situated in the heart of the Corinthian marketplace near the government offices. That platform was discovered in 1935—the exact place and the actual stones where one of Paul's trials unfolded. Gallio found no violation of Roman law or custom by Paul and threw the case out of court.

▼ THE JUDGMENT PLATFORM discovered in Corinth where legal cases were decided and where athletes received their crowns for victory. Paul certainly had this platform in mind when he wrote about every Christian's final evaluation by Jesus—"we must all appear before the judgment seat [bema] of Christ" (2 Corinthians 5:10).

▲ Paul's final imprisonment was in the dungeon of the Mamertine prison in Rome.

◄ NERO WAS THE ROMAN EMPEROR who ultimately condemned both Paul and Peter to death for their allegiance to Jesus as Lord. He ruled the Roman Empire from AD 54 to 68—a reign that ended with his suicide.

◄ MOSAIC OF A ROMAN GRAIN SHIP, the kind that Paul sailed on during his trip to Rome. In a fierce storm, the sailors threw the cargo overboard, but the ship still broke apart and wrecked off the island of Malta (Acts 27–28).

▲ WE'VE READ THE STORY IN ACTS of Paul and Silas singing hymns of praise in the prison at Philippi (Acts 16:25). Tour guides in Philippi today will point to this ancient cell as the place where Paul and Silas were locked away.

PHOTO CREDITS

All maps are © Mosaic Graphics

1–Digging Up the Bible

Golden Bowl	Erich Lessing/Art Resource, NY
Sermon on the Mount	Erich Lessing/Art Resource, NY
Dead Sea Scroll	© Topham/The Image Works
Xerxes	Giraudon/Art Resource, NY
Augustus Caesar	© ARPL/HIP/The Image Works

2–Do These Discoveries Prove the Bible Is True?

Megiddo ivory box	Z. Radovan/www.BibleLandPictures.com
Hebrew seal	Z. Radovan/www.BibleLandPictures.com
Roman slave tag	© Topham/The Image Works
Archaeologists at work	© AAAC/Topham/The Image Works
Qumran jar	© 2008 by Zondervan
Baal	Erich Lessing/Art Resource, NY

3–Babylonian Flood Story

Gilgamesh epic tablet	Z. Radovan/www.BibleLandPictures.com
Stone Gilgamesh	Erich Lessing/Art Resource, NY
Michelangelo's flood	Scala/Art Resource, NY
Mt. Ararat	Z. Radovan/www.BibleLandPictures.com
Deucalion and Pyyrha painting	www.pintura.aut.org

4–Royal Treasures of UR

Goat	© Topham/The Image Works
Royal banner	© Topham/The Image Works
Royal game	Erich Lessing/Art Resource, NY
Ziggurat	© Topham/The Image Works
Great tower	Snark/Art Resource, NY
Headdress of Puabi	Werner Forman/Art Resource, NY

5–Ebla: Living Like a Canaanite

Tel Mardikh	Erich Lessing/Art Resource, NY
Tablet from Ebla	Erich Lessing/Art Resource, NY
Gold-plated, wooden figure	Erich Lessing/Art Resource, NY
Sodom and Gomorrah	Alinari/Art Resource, NY
Salt deposits	Erich Lessing/Art Resource, NY

6–Pharaoh Hardened His Heart

Cartouche of Ramses	© ARPL/HIP/The Image Works
Brick-making mural	Erich Lessing/Art Resource, NY
Tuthmose III	Erich Lessing/Art Resource, NY
Ramses II and Queen	© Topham/The Image Works
Amenhotep II	© CM Dixon/HIP/The Image Works
Egyptian soldiers	Borromeo/Art Resource, NY

7–Out of Egypt

Hieroglyphics	Z. Radovan/www.BibleLandPictures.com
Shishak inscription	Erich Lessing/Art Resource, NY
Moses leading Israel	Scala/Art Resource, NY
Pyramids	© 1999-2008 Phoenix Data Systems
Flight to Egypt	He Qi
Menerptah's stele	Z. Radovan/www.BibleLandPictures.com

8–The Hebrews Are Coming! (Amarna Letters)

Amarna letter	© AAAC/Topham/The Image Works
Akhenaten	© AAAC/Topham/The Image Works
Ancient scribes	© AAAC/Topham/The Image Works
The Taking of Jericho painting	The Jewish Museum, NY/Art Resource, NY
Nefertiti	Courtesy of Wikimedia Commons
Cuneiform close-up	Todd Bolen/www.BiblePlaces.com

9–Jericho's Walls

Aerial view of Jericho	Z. Radovan/www.BibleLandPictures.com
Skull with plaster	Scala/Art Resource, NY
Bronze panel	Scala/Art Resource, NY
Jordan River	Erich Lessing/Art Resource, NY
Storejars of grain	Todd Bolen/www.BiblePlaces.com

10–No Other Gods

Astarte	Scala/Art Resource, NY
Calf	Z. Radovan/www.BibleLandPictures.com
Edomite goddess	Z. Radovan/www.BibleLandPictures.com
Megiddo high place	© Topham/The Image Works
Solomon adoring idols	Scala/Art Resource, NY
Reshef	Erich Lessing/Art Resource, NY
Dagon	© C. Walker/Topham/The Image Works
Adoration of Calf	Scala/Art Resource, NY

11–Hunting for Hittites

Borgazkoy	Scala/Art Resource, NY
Royal prince in nurse's arms	Sonia Halliday Photographs
David and Uriah	The Pierpont Morgan Library/ Art Resource, NY
Hittite treaty	Erich Lessing/Art Resource, NY
Hittite soldier	© Topham/The Image Works

12–Mythic King or Man of God?

Aramaic inscription	Z. Radovan/www.BibleLandPictures.com
Hazael	Erich Lessing/Art Resource, NY
Gate of Dan	Todd Bolen/www.BiblePlaces.com
Altar at Dan	Z. Radovan/www.BibleLandPictures.com
Ivory showing harp	Erich Lessing/Art Resource, NY
Sling stones	Michael Luddeni

13–Finding the Philistines

Ekron inscription	Z. Radovan/www.BibleLandPictures.com
Dagger	© David Rubinger/CORBIS
Portrait of Philistines	Todd Bolen/www.BiblePlaces.com
Goliath defeated	Scala/Art Resource, NY
Samson	The Jewish Museum, NY/ Art Resource, NY
Philistine pottery	Z. Radovan/www.BibleLandPictures.com
Philistine coffin	Z. Radovan/www.BibleLandPictures.com

14–Solomon's Temple

The house of the Lord tablet	Associated Press
Jehoash tablet	Getty Images/Handout
Inscribed pottery	Z. Radovan/www.BibleLandPictures.com
Solomon dedicates temple	Image Select/Art Resource, NY
Arad temple	Todd Bolen/www.BiblePlaces.com
God's holy name	Leningrad Codex

15–The Lost Ark

Dome of the Rock interior	Erich Lessing/Art Resource, NY
Ark model	Z. Radovan/www.BibleLandPictures.com
Anubis	© Dr. James C. Martin. The Cairo Museum. Cairo, Egypt. Photographed by permission.
David dancing	Scala/Art Resource, NY
Ethiopian monk	© Wolfgang Rattay/Reuters/Corbis
Dome of the Rock	© William D. Mounce

16–Solomon's Cities

Stable at Megiddo	Erich Lessing/Art Resource, NY
Aerial of Hazor	Todd Bolen/www.www.BiblePlaces.com
Large, vaulted areas	Associated Press
Assyrian chariot	Z. Radovan/www.BibleLandPictures.com
Megiddo gate	Z. Radovan/www.BibleLandPictures.com
David in Jerusalem gate	The Pierpont Morgan Library/ Art Resource, NY

17–The Moabite Stone

Moabite stone	Réunion des Musées Nationaux/ Art Resource, NY
Chemosh	Erich Lessing/Art Resource, NY
Moab landscape	Todd Bolen/www.BiblePlaces.com
Ruth gleaning	Scala/Art Resource, NY

Omri's palace — Z. Radovan/www.BibleLandPictures.com
Moabite inscription — Photograph by Bruce and Kenneth Zuckerman, West Semitic Research. Courtesy Department of Antiquities, Jordan.

18–A Buried City

Baal — Erich Lessing/Art Resource, NY
Elijah challenging Ahab — © ARPL/Topham/The Image Works
Asherah — Z. Radovan/www.BibleLandPictures.com
El — © Gianni Dagli Orti/Corbis
Ivory head — Giraudon/Art Resource, NY
Excavations at Ugarit — © Charles & Josette Lenars/Corbis

19–Authorized Access Only

Signet ring — Z. Radovan/www.BibleLandPictures.com
Winged scarab — Z. Radovan/www.BibleLandPictures.com
Baruch seal — Z. Radovan/www.BibleLandPictures.com
Baruch writing prophecies — Alinari/Art Resource, NY
Jasper seal — Z. Radovan/www.BibleLandPictures.com
Sealed scroll — Z. Radovan/www.BibleLandPictures.com

20–The City No One Could Find

Winged bull — © AAAC/Topham/The Image Works
Reconstructed walls of Nineveh — © AAAC/Topham/The Image Works
Cunieform tablet — Todd Bolen/www.BiblePlaces.com
Assyrian soldiers — © The British Museum/HIP/The Image Works
Dying lion — © The British Museum/HIP/The Image Works
Hunting with hounds — © The British Museum/HIP/The Image Works
Nahum predicts destruction — © The British Library/HIP/The Image Works

21–Snapshot of an Old Testament King

Jehu bows — Z. Radovan/www.BibleLandPictures.com
Shalmaneser's monument — HIP/Art Resource, NY
Jehu's servants — Z. Radovan/www.BibleLandPictures.com
Shalmaneser III — Z. Radovan/www.BibleLandPictures.com
Henry Layard — © Topham/The Image Works

22–War with Assyria

Battle — Z. Radovan/www.BibleLandPictures.com
Sennacherib drawing — © Bettmann/CORBIS
Angel defeats Assyrians — Erich Lessing/Art Resource, NY
Lachish ruins — Todd Bolen/www.BiblePlaces.com

23–Northern Kingdom Destroyed

Sargon II — Erich Lessing/Art Resource, NY
Samaria under seige — © Historical Picture Archive/Corbis Photographer: Philip de Bay
Winged bull — © Trustees of the British Museum
Sargon annals — © Topham/The Image Works
Head of Sargon — Erich Lessing/Art Resource, NY
Tombs of Nimrud — D. G. Youkhanna/Assyrian International News Agency www.aina.org

24–Hezekiah's Tunnel

Tunnel and pool — Z. Radovan/www.BibleLandPictures.com
Inscription — Z. Radovan/www.BibleLandPictures.com
Hezekiah sculpture — Z. Radovan/www.BibleLandPictures.com
Tunnel — Z. Radovan/www.BibleLandPictures.com

25–Sennacherib's Prism

Taylor's prism — Art Resource, NY
Spoils of war — Erich Lessing/Art Resource, NY
Sennacherib — Z. Radovan/www.BibleLandPictures.com
Broad wall — Z. Radovan/www.BibleLandPictures.com
Lachish ruins — © 1995–1999 Phoenix Data Systems

26–Lachish Letters

Broken pottery — Erich Lessing/Art Resource, NY
Blind Zedekiah — © Topham/The Image Works
Babylonian chronicle — © The Trustees of the British Museum
Nebuchadnezzar — © Bettmann/CORBIS
Fiery furnace — © Mallett Gallery, London, UK / The Bridgeman Art Library
Nebo-Sarsekim tablet — The Daily Telegraph/Ian Jones

27–Mistaken about Daniel

Prayer of Nabonidus — © The Trustees of the British Museum
Statue of Nabonidus — HIP/Art Resource, NY
Handwriting on wall — Art Resource, NY
Nebuchadnezzer brick — © The Trustees of the British Museum
Chronicle of Nabonidus — © The Trustees of the British Museum

28–Prophecy Fulfilled!

Tomb of Cyrus — Z. Radovan/www.BibleLandPictures.com
Cyrus sculpture — © Charles & Josette Lenars/CORBIS
Xanthos stele NW012604 — © Nik Wheeler/CORBIS
Silver amulet — Z. Radovan/www.BibleLandPictures.com
Jehoiachin tablet — Bildarchiv Preussischer Kulturbesitz/Art Resource,NY
Cyrus cylinder — HIP/Art Resource, NY

29–Cliffside Carving

Henry Rawlinson — Getty Images
Cuneiform writing — Z. Radovan/www.BibleLandPictures.com
Xerxes relief — Giraudon/Art Resource, NY
Behistun carving — SEF/Art Resource, NY
Xerxes and Esther — Erich Lessing/Art Resource, NY

30–Herod: Murderer, Dreamer, King

Aerial of Masada — Z. Radovan/www.BibleLandPictures.com
Aerial of Herodium — Z. Radovan/www.BibleLandPictures.com
Machaerus — Todd Bolen/www.www.BiblePlaces.com
John the Baptist beheaded — Erich Lessing/Art Resource, NY
Slaughter of infants — Alinari/Art Resource, NY
Herod's palace, Citadel — Z. Radovan/www.BibleLandPictures.com
Agrippa coin — Z. Radovan/www.BibleLandPictures.com
Caesarea Philippi — Z. Radovan/www.BibleLandPictures.com

31–Herod's Temple

Western wall — © 1999-2008 Phoenix Data Systems
Dome of the Rock — Z. Radovan/www.BibleLandPictures.com
Sundial — Z. Radovan/www.BibleLandPictures.com
Arch of Titus — Werner Forman/Art Resource, NY
Herod viewing temple plans — Snark/Art Resource, NY
Boy Jesus in temple — Erich Lessing/Art Resource, NY
Model of temple — © AAAC/Topham/The Image Works
Copper scroll — Photograph by Bruce and Kenneth Zuckerman, West Semitic Research. Courtesy Department of Antiquities, Jordan.
Wailing wall — Z. Radovan/www.BibleLandPictures.com

32–Jews Only

Warning sign — Z. Radovan/www.BibleLandPictures.com
Red-lettered warning sign — Z. Radovan/www.BibleLandPictures.com
Sign from second temple — Z. Radovan/www.BibleLandPictures.com
Christ with religious leaders — Erich Lessing/Art Resource, NY
Bone box — © The British Museum/HIP/The Image Works
Court of Gentiles — © 1999–2008 Phoenix Data Systems

33–The Jesus Boat

Boat — Z. Radovan/www.BibleLandPictures.com
Boat during preservation — © John Berry/The Image Works
Fishermen with nets — Z. Radovan/www.BibleLandPictures.com
Boat mosaic — Z. Radovan/www.BibleLandPictures.com
Peter walking on water — Scala/Art Resource, NY

34–The Bible Jesus Read

Isaiah scroll	Z. Radovan/ www.BibleLandPictures.com
Qumran cave	Todd Bolen/www.BiblePlaces.com
Scribe writing	Todd Bolen/www.BiblePlaces.com
Stylus	The Schøyen Collection MS 5095/ 3, Oslo and London
Scriptorium	Z. Radovan/ www.BibleLandPictures.com
Mountain of the leap	Z. Radovan/ www.BibleLandPictures.com

35–Pontius Pilate

Pilate inscription	Z. Radovan/ www.BibleLandPictures.com
Pilate coin	JerusalemCoins.com
Caesarea Maritima	Todd Bolen/www.BiblePlaces.com
Pilate presenting Jesus	Alinari/Art Resource, NY
Ecce Homo arch	Z. Radovan/ www.BibleLandPictures.com

36–Crucifixion

Ankle bone	Z. Radovan/ www.BibleLandPictures.com
Paving stone	Z. Radovan/ www.BibleLandPictures.com
Roman Scourge	Illustrated by Mark Sheeres
Family tomb	© www.gregschneider.com
Golgotha	Z. Radovan/ www.BibleLandPictures.com
Via Dolorosa	Z. Radovan/ www.BibleLandPictures.com
Crucifixion painting	Réunion des Musées Nationaux/ Art Resource, NY

37–Everyday Treasures

Stone jars	Z. Radovan/ www.BibleLandPictures.com
Sandals	Z. Radovan/ www.BibleLandPictures.com
Goat skin containers	Z. Radovan/ www.BibleLandPictures.com
Limestone tablet	Z. Radovan/ www.BibleLandPictures.com
Alabaster jars	Erich Lessing/Art Resource, NY
Mary annointing Jesus	Erich Lessing/Art Resource, NY

38–Famous Faces

Aretas IV coin	Z. Radovan/ www.BibleLandPictures.com
Augustus coin	Z. Radovan/ www.BibleLandPictures.com
Claudius coin	Z. Radovan/ www.BibleLandPictures.com
Widow's mite coin	JerusalemCoins.com
Agrippa I coin	Z. Radovan/ www.BibleLandPictures.com
Herod the Great coin	JerusalemCoins.com
Tiberius denarius	JerusalemCoins.com
Widow's mite mosaic	Erich Lessing/Art Resource, NY

39–Bone Boxes

James ossuary small	Photo by DeAnna Putnam
James ossuary large	Photo by DeAnna Putnam
James ossuary inscription	Photo by DeAnna Putnam
Herod family tomb	Erich Lessing/Art Resource, NY
Jesus before Caiaphas	Art Resource, NY
Caiaphas bone box	Z. Radovan/ www.BibleLandPictures.com

40–Peter's House

Walls of first century room	Erich Lessing/Art Resource, NY
Strong foundation	Z. Radovan/ www.BibleLandPictures.com
St. Peter's Basilica, Rome	© Topham/The Image Works
Peter's crucifixion	Planet Art

41–Sightseeing in Corinth

Erastus inscription	Z. Radovan/ www.BibleLandPictures.com
Corinth synagogue inscription	Z. Radovan/ www.BibleLandPictures.com
Temple of Apollo	Z. Radovan/ www.BibleLandPictures.com
Corinth meat market inscription	Z. Radovan/ www.BibleLandPictures.com
Lachaion road	Erich Lessing/Art Resource, NY
Runners	Erich Lessing/Art Resource, NY

42–Touring Ephesus

Ephesus theater	Z. Radovan/ www.BibleLandPictures.com
Artemis	Erich Lessing/Art Resource, NY
Commercial agora	Todd Bolen/www.BiblePlaces.com
Temple of Artemis	Vanni/Art Resource, NY
St. John's basilia	Todd Bolen/www.BiblePlaces.com
Apostle John	© Hermitage, St. Petersburg, Russia/ The Bridgeman Art Library

43–Paul in Trouble

Bema in Corinth	Erich Lessing/Art Resource, NY
Philippi prison	Todd Bolen/www.BiblePlaces.com
Mamertine prison	Erich Lessing/Art Resource, NY
Mosaic of grain ship	© AAAC/Topham/ The Image Works
Nero coin	Z. Radovan/ www.BibleLandPictures.com
Paul lowered in basket	Erich Lessing/Art Resource, NY
Damascus wall	Galen R. Frysinger